UPGRADE

Celebrating
30 Years of Publishing
in India

UPGRADE

The Not-So-Subtle Art of Moving Up in Life and Career

Priyesh Khanna | Alasdair Ross

HARPER
BUSINESS

An Imprint of HarperCollins *Publishers*

First published as *The Business of You* in the United Kingdom by
Celebrity Publishers in 2020

This edition published in India by Harper Business 2023
An imprint of HarperCollins *Publishers*
4th Floor, Tower A, Building No. 10, DLF Cyber City,
DLF Phase II, Gurugram, Haryana – 122002
www.harpercollins.co.in

2 4 6 8 10 9 7 5 3 1

P-ISBN: 978-93-5699-316-7
E-ISBN: 978-93-5699-319-8

Typeset in 11.5/15.2 Adobe Garamond at
Manipal Technologies Limited, Manipal

Printed and bound at
Manipal Technologies Limited, Manipal

This book is produced from independently certified FSC® paper to ensure
responsible forest management.

To my father, the first inspirational, go-getter leader in my life; my mother who taught me unashamed affection. Rajiv, Rosy and, of course, beloved Anshu for helping me keep it real.
Finally, Aaryan, Anika, Aarti and all the kids in the family: I wrote this book for you. I hope this brings you happiness in your journeys, my darlings.
— Priyesh Khanna

Contents

How to Use This Book

The book centres on the belief that most of us want to be successful in all aspects of life, including our careers. However, being proficient at the tasks we're assigned is only one aspect of our professional performance. To reach your ultimate goal, you will need to:

- Align your priorities with those of the organization you work for
- Utilize your team members' skills correctly, both inside and outside the firm
- Remain in control of your emotions
- Go above and beyond to deliver on projects within defined deadlines
- Refine your communication and messaging skills

In many ways, the more we manage ourselves as a business with a product—one that needs nurturing and promoting for the betterment of our clients—the better placed we are in building a network of trust and reputation for high performance. This book helps to build that way of thinking by providing powerful methods and real-life examples of achievement.

Upgrade is arranged in four parts, each with its individual aim to strengthen the key dimensions that make up the habits, mindsets and actions of highly successful corporate performers. We have written the book so that each chapter can be read independently, allowing the reader to focus on areas of particular interest where needed.

However, for the most effective journey, we recommend reading the book in the order presented. For example, it makes sense that you need to be confident you can communicate well and deliver what you promise before you can build a strong client base or ask for a promotion. Therefore, reading the chapters on communication, delegation and managing projects should come before client-relationship management.

Foreword

Why is it better to not be so subtle if you want to upgrade yourself?

Because your success, satisfaction and the metaphor for achieving your goals—obtaining that sought-after big promotion—is in your hands, and if it is a priority for you, then why beat about the bush?

For some, becoming a great leader and leading others seems unimaginable and out of reach. Many people lack the confidence, know-how and strategies to achieve their goals. Instead, they dwell in a place that is neither inspiring nor fulfilling. *Upgrade* is all about changing your current beliefs and approach to work and transforming these into a master plan that brings about genuine, fast-paced career progression.

The pairing of Priyesh Khanna and Alasdair Ross—one that ticks off many of the book's objectives in itself—delivers a toolkit of experience, guidance and exercises for the reader to work through as they journey to the top. From clear communication and project management advice to client relationships, networking and creating a knockout curriculum vitae (CV), there is little that Khanna and Ross have not covered.

This is the perfect read for anyone who has the yearning to ascend the career ladder but also wants to tick off multiple goals and achievements along the way. Read *Upgrade*, and the journey to your upgrade will get a whole lot shorter.

Anke Raufuss
Partner, McKinsey and Company

Introduction

Upgrade is a real-world insight into what it takes to succeed in today's highly competitive corporate environment. It provides practical-development and acceleration techniques drawn from the authors' first-hand experience and shares methods for achieving absolute career advancement through proactive, collaborative and leadership behaviours.

This book is for those who aspire to reach the peak of their career while simultaneously leading fulfilling personal lives. Rapid economic development in some of the world's biggest emerging markets has injected millions of ambitious, well-educated young people into the global workforce. Many complete their studies abroad and begin their careers at large multinational corporations, where competition for senior roles is intense and the route to the top is not always easy to establish. It can be just as challenging for young people in the developed world, striving to build their careers in a complex, globalized labour market with ever-shrinking opportunities on their home turf.

Upgrade assumes its readers are smart, qualified, hard-working and ambitious, but it also recognizes that navigating the corporate hierarchy requires more than just these qualities. The book aims to provide an armoury of principles, techniques and behaviours that will shorten the path to greatness and make the journey more satisfying.

Young professionals are trained to compete ruthlessly for advancement, while TV and social media entice them to engage in cynical—and ultimately fruitless—self-promotion. This approach leaves most frustrated and unaware of their potential. This book presents a more practical and effective way of achieving career success by winning support from colleagues, communicating more effectively across the organization and gaining the trust of senior staff. The method relies on bringing out an individual's innate talents without sacrificing other aspects of their lives. There can be no guarantees, but a combination of collaboration, trust and good service can bring great satisfaction and improve the odds of success.

At its core, *Upgrade* aims to:

- Guide individuals through every stage of their progression
- Help them identify the quickest route to the top
- Ensure they continue to prosper once they reach their destination

My Not-So-Subtle Upgrade Story

by Priyesh Khanna

Like many, my journey began as an IT programmer. The first project was writing test scripts for a call centre system, which ultimately led me to become a global managing director working for top-tier international banks.

There were many learnings I picked up on this unpredictable road, but I'm sure others would have had similar experiences. The difference is that I recognized repeated patterns in successful leaders. Sometimes, I broke these down into easily applicable standalone methods; at other times, I connected these into compound techniques that cumulatively increased personal impact and the probability of success.

I first wrote these down for my kids so they could have a more fruitful, smoother life, as every father would wish. This is my true legacy to them and evidence of my utmost belief in the merit of these not-so-subtle ways to accelerate one's personal goals.

One turning point in my career was particularly significant. As a junior manager, I was doing relatively well running one of the largest global projects for a tier-1 bank. I was content that in good time, it would be my turn to be promoted to the next level, which was to become a 'director'. I wasn't proactively managing this, just working hard on outstanding delivery. That should be enough, surely?

One day I watched another person being promoted above me, and it was someone I had hired and several years junior to me!

It was a cold February morning in New York, and I picked up the phone to share my fury with my boss in London. He was a calm soul and told me the problem was one of 'visibility'. What the hell did he mean? I was charged with delivering one of the most important initiatives for the firm—how could I be invisible to the powers that be? It was an eye-opener.

I was key to a mission-critical project that had visibility up to the board level of the bank, but I was clearly doing something wrong. After getting over the shock, disbelief and anger, I started identifying the gaps between me and my seniors at the next level—the directors.

This began a journey of transformation—from being a good delivery manager to a leader—at first of myself, then others. Though, initially, it was a hard pill to swallow, there were many gaps to fill between the manager I was and the leader I needed to become—some subtle but many not-so-subtle!

That following year, in addition to successfully landing the big delivery, I refined my visibility by building relationships and trust. I took charge of aligning expectations with my seniors and shortly afterwards, I got my prized promotion. I was also compensated handsomely for my hard work and perseverance.

To this day, I continue to observe, listen and refine myself. It's a great habit to have—continuous learning from leaders all around you.

There is something special that defines you and makes you unique. We need to be self-aware to appreciate this, but to do well and be promoted, we also need to demonstrate the traits others value highly in our organizations. This is the not-so-subtle art of getting on in life and your career.

A not-so-subtle experience that influenced me early on in my career was that of standing on my bank's trading floor in the summer of 2002. The room was the size of an Olympic stadium, cluttered with multicoloured computer screens and traders shouting bids over each other as if their lives depended on it. Just when you thought nothing could calm this rowdy lot, a sudden hush spread as Bob Diamond, then CEO of Barclays Capital Investment Bank, appeared in the middle of the floor. In a booming voice, he spoke about the bank's quarterly performance and future strategy with his global team of twenty-thousand-odd trading, banking, technology and support staff. It was like a call to battle—the founding father of one of the world's most successful investment banks driving home the facts underpinning our success and painting a vision that left many of us with that tingling feeling of honour, privilege and a thirst to take the bank to the next level.

Time and again, I experienced Bob's straight-talking yet mesmerizingly charismatic communication. Years later, I observed Barack Obama, Steve Jobs and other lesser known but incredibly successful corporate leaders use similar ingredients to rally their audiences. What was the secret? Was this a formula by design or merely a coincidence? Either way, it was enough for me to know that there was a priceless technique here to uncover and utilize.

Along my unpredictable journey from an entry-level graduate to managing director, I've been fortunate to learn an array of leadership techniques from senior executives and specialist coaches within the corporate ecosystem. Combined with my first-hand experience of what works and what doesn't, these methods have become a potent antidote to obstacles and the foundation of my success. Now, I want to shine a light on others to help them realize their potential and better navigate their own game of corporate snakes and ladders.

Of course, I appreciate the benefits that come with a successful career like money, achievement, self-respect and pride. However, it was a simpler truth that drove my development of these tools for myself and others. The fact is, we spend most of our waking lives at work. If we don't love what we do, we're setting ourselves up to be unhappy forever. To me, that's not just scary; it's totally unacceptable. Being successful—and being recognized for that success—is a pillar of our day-to-day satisfaction and peace of mind. This book was born from a wish to provide tools to anyone who feels they can achieve more and thrive and, consequently, become a happier person.

There have been many instances of bright, enthusiastic individuals who somehow stalled in their careers or felt there was a more efficient way to progress. Often, all it required was the untangling of a few mental knots to unleash their full potential. As an example, I knew a mid-level bank manager—let's call him Jim for the sake of data protection. Jim hit a career ceiling and wasn't rising to his management's expectations, no matter how hard he tried. It was looking increasingly doubtful that he would ever be promoted again. He was concerned his superiors would overlook him in favour of a budding junior or, worse still, try and find a way to squeeze him out of the business. Naturally, with two children, a mortgage and years of hard work invested, it was playing on his mind and putting a strain on his marriage.

Jim came to me for a little advice—off the record. It became evident to me that he was the primary bottleneck within his team. He needed to learn who to empower in his team—and how—so they could collectively multiply their value to the organization. He also needed to be able to manage his superior's expectations, so they had rock-solid faith in his product. His own desire for the highest quality and inability to connect with the powers that be were pushing him and his team to the back of the queue.

Thankfully, he was humble enough to swallow the medicine I prescribed, accepting he needed to change. By applying simple yet powerful techniques related to team-work management, delegation and upward engagement, his career trajectory took a turn for the better. Six months later, his boss—who just so happens to be a peer of mine—approached me to ask if I would be a referee to support Jim's promotion.

I can't express to you how rewarding it was for me to hear this.

I have many diverse success stories to tell, demonstrating how the use of personal-effectiveness techniques has changed the lives of people like Jim. Although I enjoy one-to-one coaching, mentoring and fireside seminars, I realized that if these tools and methods could be made more widely available, so many others in Jim's position could accelerate their contributions and reap the rewards early in their careers. It was a huge turning point for me, and was the moment I first put pen to paper.

I was fortunate enough to meet Alasdair Ross, a well-established journalist and senior editor with The Economist Group for over twenty years. Alasdair showed a great appreciation for my concepts, agreeing to partner with me and add his perspectives, as well as his world-class writing style. We hope this fusion makes for a compelling read that provides powerful armaments for the reader to become more efficient at work. We aspire to help create a more productive, fulfilling workplace experience for corporate employees and their firms.

Chapter Plan

Part One: The Aspirant's Toolkit

In this first part of the book, we aim to build a solid foundation for delivering great results. We provide techniques to communicate, delegate, deliver projects, control emotions and manage the most precious commodity—time.

Communicating 360

Your ideas may be good, but they don't really take off until you convey them clearly and persuasively. This chapter looks at techniques for getting your message across and increasing the odds of a favourable hearing. We provide a case study of a conversation that rarely turns out as you hope it would—salary negotiation.

Delivery: Delegation

Far too many ambitious people believe that to progress, they must demonstrate they can do everything. Successful leaders understand they can multiply their capacity many times over by sharing tasks, as well as introducing skills they may not possess into the equation. This chapter shows how to delegate by building partnerships rather than just handing out duties. A real-life example looks at a team working together to satisfy a demanding banking regulator.

Delivery: Managing Projects

No business thrives without change. If it did, your route to the corner office would require little more than repeating your to-do list more diligently than your rivals. Businesses are driven forward by individuals who bring the right kind of change in the most effective way. In this chapter, we look at key techniques for ensuring you complete the projects you are given within the allotted deadline and with the desired results.

Controlling Your Emotions

Ambition and stress go together like speed and wind resistance, but unless you have control over your emotions, they can bring you to an abrupt halt. This chapter looks at developing an awareness of your emotional responses to a challenge and shaping them to help you succeed. It isn't just about performing under pressure; it's about using pressure to perform better. We take the reader into a management meeting to demonstrate our philosophy.

Managing Your Time

Teamwork and delegation are effective ways to multiply capacity; nevertheless, there are only so many hours in the day. Making the most of your time means spending it wisely. This chapter looks at finding the right balance between doing what you love and taking care of routine jobs, making game-changing decisions and taking time off. We look at how to defeat some of the most prevalent time-killers, punctuate your day with rewarding bursts of achievement and dedicate time to those tasks that will further your rise to the corner office.

Part Two: Building Trust

With these essential tools under your belt, we turn to methods of nurturing trustworthy relationships with your clients, your network and those who ultimately decide the trajectory of your career—your superiors.

Managing Client Relationships

During your rise to the top, you will probably find yourself interacting with both internal and external clients. Undoubtedly, this is a rewarding aspect of your career and one you should seek out wherever possible. In this chapter, we apply a few choice sales techniques to help you build successful commercial and professional relationships. These include mapping who your clients are, gaining their attention, understanding their needs, determining where and how to engage them, and building a fruitful relationship.

Building a Network

With achievement comes recognition, but don't leave it to chance. Your odds of progression will rise as you become more renowned, and you can expedite the process by nurturing a network of people who know what you can do. This chapter outlines ways to make yourself more prominent inside and outside your organization using professional, social and virtual connections. We look at how to increase the equity in your trust bank and build your network—first within your own team, then the wider organization, and finally, the world beyond. Then, when opportunity knocks, it won't just be you who is listening.

Managing Up

Once you have a team of your own, you will be judged on your ability to rally your troops and encourage them to deliver on every mission. However, if you want to move up, relationship management can't stop there. As you advance, the person best placed to champion your cause will often be your manager, so fostering a relationship with them is key. This chapter looks at how to build an effective and productive relationship with your boss, based on shared goals and agreed priorities.

Part Three: The Personal Entrepreneur

To be a true professional, you need to operate proficiently and commercially. This section of the book focuses on how you should market yourself and develop your enterprise. We introduce a mindset shift to help you transform from a follower into an owner and leader.

Selling Yourself

Whether you're looking for your first job or want to climb another rung on the career ladder, you will face two ritual trials: the CV and the interview. In this chapter, we set out a practical guide to acing these fundamental tests. You will need a CV that tells a compelling story, focusing less on titles and more on the things you've done. You will need to persuade your interviewer that you understand the attributes required for the job and that you have them. We add a note for school-leavers who often need to underpin their proposal with a persuasive origin story.

The Business of You

The best way to be recognized as a credible candidate for a senior role is to demonstrate a degree of aptitude for it before you apply. In this chapter, we look at how to approach your career as if it were any other entrepreneurial endeavour. We discuss how to apply the lessons you've learnt so far to serve your clients, encouraging them to seek you out and sing your praises. These individuals will become your champions as you progress.

Married to the Job: The Role of HR

As you build your networks and partnerships, both within and outside the organization, you should be aware that there is one department whose mission is to help you make the best possible contribution to the company's success. We explain how Human Resources acts as the marriage counsellor of your employment contract, for better or worse.

Part Four: Journey's End, Journey's Beginning

The final chapter takes workplace skills to the highest levels, sharing key traits that define today's successful corporate leaders, that is, those who occupy the proverbial 'corner office'. The very best in the corporate world use these techniques to inspire, influence and focus colleagues while still managing their personal and professional lives effectively.

The View from the Corner Office

So far, we've guided you along the journey to the corner office, but what happens when you get there? The big lessons you learnt in the previous ten chapters still apply, but now, you need to demonstrate leadership qualities. This chapter lays out six key behavioural traits that the most successful managing directors (MDs) share, from spotting and riding the wave in your industry to maintaining a fulfilling personal life. We look at what differentiates a leader from a manager and how leading can help you stay successful long after you reach the top.

All the methods in this book are based on solid management foundations, some of which you may have seen before. However, it is the combination of these techniques that makes for a powerful concoction of continued achievement and success.

We present a bonus chapter called 'Zoomify Your Career' to help develop your leadership presence online. With most of us working on Zoom, Teams and other video conferencing platforms—often from home—it is important to know which new traits are needed, which ones need to be adapted, and the ones that should be protected to be successful. 'Zoomify Your Career' provides insights to ensure online working doesn't get in the way of your 'upgrade' ambitions.

A final word before the main feature. *Upgrade* aims to promote ideas that enable high performance in a way that drives a positive and proactive organizational culture. For this reason, it can be of great benefit to corporates and individuals alike, so feel free to share it openly; after all, a more effective and successful organization will provide a wider, more enriching platform for your career.

Now, let the transformation begin!

PART ONE

THE ASPIRANT'S TOOLKIT

1

Communicating 360

- *Do you ever feel tongue-tied when speaking with someone in a senior position?*
- *Do you sometimes say too much or too little?*
- *Have people told you that you need to work on your communication style?*
- *Are you concerned that you are not getting your message across?*
- *Do you worry your listeners don't understand you clearly enough?*

There are plenty of jobs where the need to communicate with colleagues and clients is of secondary importance, but if you're reading this book, those jobs probably aren't for you. To do well in a large organization staffed with smart and powerful people, you'll often need to be able to inform and persuade those around you. Poor communicators rarely reach positions of seniority, or if they do, they don't tend to hold on to them for very long.

Even the best ideas can fail if they aren't conveyed clearly and persuasively. On the same token, smooth talkers can make the worst ideas sound great, although they often get found out after a failure or two. If you're unable to display the knowledge and skills that set you apart, even your most enthusiastic advocate will struggle to promote you. No one is persuaded by an argument that is flawed in its logic. Ambiguity, imprecision and reticence are your enemies when it comes to being listened to rather than just heard.

Effective communication helps you land your message. It requires clarity of thought and a structured approach. Think of it like a pilot bringing down a plane smoothly, much to the delight of their passengers.

In *Lord of the Flies*, William Golding's classic novel of adolescent survival, the castaways pass around a conch shell to signify whose turn it is to speak. Unfortunately, while holding the conch provides speakers with a platform, only the most persuasive turn this into influence. For Piggy, the bespectacled anti-hero of the book, it's simply an opportunity for more assertive speakers to steal the spotlight and impose their ideas.

Corporate communication may seem a world away from savage kids marooned on a deserted island, but it is surprisingly common for business meetings to be dominated by the loudest voices, all contesting for speaking time. This atmosphere prizes volume over logic and encourages off-the-cuff assertions designed to grab attention rather than carefully considered proposals. Such meetings rarely result in the smartest ideas being adopted, or their proponents being recognized. However, even in such circumstances, a clear message expressed in the right language will resonate and elicit a response.

The most effective leaders use three foundational techniques to get their message across:

1. Speak with purpose and clarity, rallying facts in support of your arguments.
2. Adapt your approach, timing and tone to your audience.
3. Confirm understanding and solicit feedback.

If you do not speak with clarity, then after a meeting that apparently ended in agreement, you may find people were actually agreeing to different things. If you fail to bring supporting facts to the conversation, you will have little defence against others who do. Your listener is more likely to give you a positive hearing if you speak in a way that is suited to the context and the expectations of your listeners. Giving your boss orders is unlikely to work!

The best way to make sure you have been understood is to summarize the outcome of the meeting aloud and invite your listeners to respond. It will bring any misunderstandings to the table and allow your listeners an opportunity to offer their thoughts.

With regard to effective communication, we are not referring to discreet steps that, if followed, will ensure your success. Rather, we are introducing techniques that work together to help you achieve your aim. Later, in this chapter and throughout the book, we will show examples of our ideology in practice.

Chew Over Your Words

To convey your message clearly, you must first understand it yourself, which requires preparation. A communicator can rarely launch into a speech without some prior thought. Spontaneous outbursts are more common at the nightmare meetings we just described, rather than being a reliable way to make the right impression.

Before we speak, it is critical to establish a clear message in our minds and plan the key arguments that will get it across. Simply put, we should engage our minds before our mouths. Doing so can be a challenge for extroverts accustomed to thinking aloud. However, the most persuasive leaders use their words carefully, sparingly and selectively.

A particularly effective method is to say the following to yourself before you speak: 'What I really want to say or ask is ...' This simple technique allows you to 'chew over your words', refine them and phrase them in a more digestible way, ensuring that when you do speak, you will be focused on the purpose of the interaction.

Imagine you have been asked what gets you up in the morning—what would you say? Posed with this question, people often point to the details of their day: taking the kids to school, heading to work and the simple pleasure of that first cup of coffee. While these may be factually correct, your listener is more likely to be inspired by a deeper motivation like your pursuit of a dream. Asking what it is you really want to say and being mindful of the person you are addressing focuses your message more effectively.

If there is something you want to communicate at the moment, say a conversation about work or home, you have a perfect opportunity to test this method. Try it out now.

The Elevator Pitch

Sometimes, finding the right words is not the problem. The more passionate and knowledgeable we are about a topic, the greater the risk that an invitation to discuss it will open our mental floodgates, unleashing a torrent of words that threatens to drown our listener. Using too many words is as damaging to our message as choosing the wrong ones. Most listeners have a limited attention span and can only absorb so much information in one sitting. In the corporate world, people often juggle a multitude of competing priorities, so the time you have to get your message across is even more limited.

Brevity and precision are vital. You must distil your message if you want it to be heard.

In common parlance, this is called the elevator pitch. Presumably, the phrase originates from America—admittedly, the 'lift' pitch doesn't have quite the same ring to it!

Imagine that you are taking a lift from the thirtieth floor to the ground level where the senior executive you're trying to persuade will leave the building. The lift is travelling at a speed of one floor per second, so you have thirty seconds to plant an irresistible idea in their mind. If you get it wrong, they will shrug and walk away. Get it right, and they will find themselves mulling it over at lunch. It will pop into their mind when they are surfing Netflix that evening. Soon, they will make time for you to lay it out in more detail; at which point, it will stand up or fall on its own merit. If you want your idea to blossom, you must first plant the seed.

Imagine your idea as a newspaper story. As any reporter knows, you need to understand your story at three separate levels: the headline, the introductory paragraph and the main body of the story. The headline performs two functions; it selects the audience by giving enough detail to signal its relevance to the reader and hooks them in by promising important information. The introductory paragraph, called the lede in reporting circles, summarizes the main points of the story and tells the reader why it matters to them. A great lede gives the reader just enough that they can skip the rest and still get the kernel of the story, though a great headline and lede should compel them to read on to the end.

When you are confronted with your potential listener in the elevator, your job is to give them the headline and the lede so they will want to come back for the full story.

The term elevator pitch is believed to originate from the world of journalism rather than business. Michael Caruso, a senior editor at *Vanity Fair*, was known to use any moment he got with

Editor-in-Chief Tina Brown to pitch his story ideas, often during the four-storey lift ride from her office to her car. His partner, fellow journalist Ilene Rosenzweig, took to greeting him with the phrase 'So, how was your elevator pitch?' True or apocryphal, this concept neatly sums up the task you face when trying to sell a big idea in a small space.

Like asking yourself 'What do I really want to say?', the elevator pitch forces us to think before we speak. In this case, we know what we want to say, but we need to compress our message into as few words as possible. Senior sales executives often adopt this technique to ensure their teams are telling a consistent story to all clients and prospects.

Your pitch may consist of a brief introduction of yourself and your company, including some detail that might be of particular interest to them. It should always include an invitation to follow up, opening the door for the next conversation.

Here are some examples of elevator pitches.

In case you bump into a client and need to make a connection with them, you could go with this:

Hi John, I'm Nisha Desai. I work for the Risk Practice at Andernal Consulting. I heard you speak at the town hall, and I was really intrigued by your perspective on inflation. I'd love to spend some time with you to understand it better. Do you think it would be possible to get thirty minutes in your diary?

And when sharing your team's recent achievements with a senior department head:

Hi Jim, I hear your team won the Holland deal— congratulations! That deserves a celebration. Maybe we could do a joint drinks outing, as we've just finished our rollout of the iLoan product in New York. Shall I organize something?

Rule of Three

Once we have constructed an elevator pitch, we may want to add more details to support it, assuming there is time to include them before we reach the ground floor. The rule of three is a useful tip for adding detail. For millennia, we have understood that delivering a message in three succinct points amplifies its effect.

Julius Caesar's description of a successful campaign 'Veni, Vidi, Vici' was an effective signal to an uppity empire that he was not to be messed with. The founders of France's Third Republic adopted the phrase 'Liberté, Égalité, Fraternité' offering a memorable and uplifting summary of the republican ideal to the wider world. As children, we were told, 'A Mars a day helps you work, rest and play!' Who could resist?

Once you start to look, you will see the rule of three operating all around you:

- Politics: Tony Blair's 'Education, education, education'
- Religion: Faith, hope and charity
- Popular culture: The good, the bad and the ugly

It can work for you too. Simply adding details as the elevator descends risks your message becoming unfocused or overwhelming. Instead, think of the three main points you want to get across. They could be about the information being shared, questions to be considered, challenges and proposals to put across, or a combination of all three. Remember to ask, 'What I really want to say is …' as you consider each point.

Once you have identified your three points, order them by their importance and relevance to the listener. To capture their attention and build trust, the first point should be the most interesting and the least likely to provoke an argument. That is not to say the other points should be boring or inaccurate, but it is important to prioritize so you get a foot in the door. You could also consider making one of the points personally interesting to the listener. 'We have ten major clients and we just opened an office in New York with a hundred employees. It's close to your building.'

The third point could aim to build an emotional connection with the listener. 'We aim to give 5 per cent of our profits to local adult education charities.' Try this out for yourself right now with something important you want to say, be it in a personal or professional context.

When it comes to sharpening our elevator pitch, we get better at picking out key details as we become more experienced. In our professional lives, we will often find ourselves pushing a single idea to several different audiences. Each time, we have an opportunity to hone the message and incorporate the feedback we receive.

Listen and Confirm

In any interaction where you are trying to get an important message across, simply giving it your best shot is not enough. You need to be sure you have been understood. Your key points may ring out as clear as a bell in your own mind but could fail to have the desired effect on your audience. Your listeners might nod in agreement, but are they agreeing with what you think you said or what they think they heard? Perhaps you have heard the saying that the best communicators are great listeners.

During and after your pitch, you need to be ready for feedback. Before the meeting, consider, 'If I were in their shoes, what would

I say or challenge?' This kind of preparation puts you in a good position to respond to feedback when it comes. Senior managers rely on this technique ahead of important meetings when ambiguity can be particularly damaging. If your audience does not provide feedback spontaneously, you should ask for it.

Speak Like a Leader

It is worth restating your understanding of what has been said and summarizing the conclusions or agreements that emerged from the conversation. That way, any gaps in understanding or ambiguities in the conclusions that have been drawn should reveal themselves. The point of delivering a message is to secure a result. If you can confirm that all are agreed on what that result is, you can be confident your pitch has achieved its goal. Your confirmation should include a follow-up plan. Leaving things open-ended can lead to uncertainty. A good project manager will suggest and agree on the next milestone.

We will now demonstrate these techniques with a real-life example.

Real-Life Example: Getting a Pay Rise

Not all meetings are about a strategic initiative or bold innovation. Some of your pitches will be far more prosaic but no less significant from a personal and professional perspective. We will use one of the most fraught pitches of all as an example: asking your boss for a pay rise—a delicate topic that needs to be handled with diplomacy, confidence and integrity.

The dangers of getting it wrong are less obvious than the rewards for getting it right. You need to be certain your performance merits greater rewards than you are already receiving.

A simple accounting exercise will help you make this judgement. First, note down the facts that support your case. For example:

- You have had glowing performance reviews this year.
- You have achieved significant goals over the past two years.
- Your role has expanded.
- You have not had a pay rise of more than 1 per cent for three years when the inflation rate is 4 per cent.
- You have been told that the market rate for people with your skills is 30 per cent higher than what you are receiving.
- You are having a second child and need the additional income.

Next, draft the elevator pitch. Remember the golden rule: 'What I really want to say is …'

> Could I ask you to consider me for a pay rise this year? Based on my role and performance, I think I'm under-market in terms of my compensation.

Remember, communicating to influence is largely about understanding your audience's standpoint, preferences and motivations. Only then can you individualize your message for their ear. In this example, you are talking to your boss. Typically, leaders prefer not to be told what decisions they should make, so couching your proposal as a polite request is more likely to get the response you want, however overdue you think the pay rise may be.

To flesh out your pitch, add colour along the three dimensions we discussed earlier:

1. The most important and least controversial of your points.
2. Something of personal interest to the listener.
3. A point that creates an emotional connection.

Given that my role has expanded to managing a global team this year, head-hunters have told me that a person of my experience is paid at least 30 per cent more in the current market. I think I've fallen behind, as I've had pay increases of 1 per cent annually for the last three years, while inflation has been running at 4 per cent. I hope the fact that my performance has been rated as 'above expectation' this year also supports my case for a pay rise. It would really help right now—I have another baby on the way.

This pitch is built on clear facts and delivered in a way that ensures the speaker is taken seriously, helping to build a case for a pay rise based on performance and market benchmarks. We are also making a case that there is a genuine need for additional income at a human level. Although the company is under no obligation to recognize personal circumstances, financial difficulties can become a significant practical challenge for a valued worker and persuade them to look for better compensation elsewhere. Remember, we are making a case for the company to pay a higher price for something they have undervalued. It is crucial to be clear in your mind that you are worth it before you ask for more money.

Finally, it is important to confirm that our message has come across as we intended and to establish the next steps. In our example, we might say:

I do appreciate that times are hard for the firm, but I hope you agree with me that this is a reasonable request given my circumstances.

It may sound like overkill, but it sends several powerful explicit and implicit messages. First, you are showing your commercial awareness of the company's financial position. Budget-holders find few things more frustrating than requests for resources with no recognition of the associated constraints. Second, you are asking for personal help and support. If the reasoning is genuine, most people will respond to a personal appeal. Finally, you are asking for an opinion, rather than simply demanding more money. You are asking your boss to agree with your case for a pay rise. If they do, it becomes harder to turn you down.

In most conversations, it is a good idea to confirm your understanding of the response and arrange a follow-up. Imagine they reply with something open-ended like this:

> We'll have to see. The firm hasn't done well this year, but I'll put it on the compensation committee in November.

You might respond with:

> Thank you, I really appreciate you taking up the fight for me. Would you mind if I put something in the diary for the end of November so I can get some indication of how things go? I'd like to plan my budget.

Typically, exact pay rise figures are not shared until the company's budget is finalized, but in this case you have at least agreed that you and your boss will discuss it further, clarifying that there are follow-up expectations. Knowing they have a meeting booked means your case is less likely to slip their mind when the compensation committee meeting takes place.

Another key consideration when communicating an important message is timing—when should you seek a conversation, so your message gets the attention it deserves? It may seem an obvious point, but it is so important that it is worth emphasizing. Senior managers are dealing with dozens of issues at once and are understandably particular about when and where various topics are discussed. We recall occasions where a topic would be raised at the end of a meeting, only to be dismissed or deferred to a time when it could be properly discussed. Ideas rarely emerge strengthened from such experiences.

Messages are also better received when the listener is in the right frame of mind. It would be best to broach the salary conversation in a situation where your boss is pleased with something you have done. They are more likely to want to hear what you have to say and resist the temptation to rush on to the next task. Holding a discussion in a semi-formal setting—over coffee, for example— amplifies the personal aspects of your request.

Is there a specific voice you should be using to get your message across? Next time you are speaking to a senior manager or leader, take note of the tone and pace of their voice.

- Do they speak quickly and repeat themselves?
- Does their voice quiver?
- Do they become breathless and stumble over words?

They likely speak with a natural tone and pace that is comfortable to them and shows a command of their words, as well as a relaxed frame of mind. Everyone gets agitated from time to time, but note how you react when you are speaking to someone whose voice betrays that they are not in control of their emotions. It puts you on your guard and elevates your own emotional state to match theirs. It can be useful when there is some urgency to be conveyed, but if you are trying to convince someone of your case or want them to take the time to give you a fair hearing, an accelerated delivery is unlikely to help.

As a rule of thumb, the tone of your voice should be respectful but confident. A key element to consider is the pace and depth of your voice. Generally, a medium pace is preferred. Too fast or rushed, and you may come across nervous. Too slow, and you might seem lethargic or even lacking in intelligence. You should also aim to avoid monotone speech and be expressive by modulating your voice subtly. Pitch fluctuation can help connect with your audience. Some of the most effective communicators are actors. If you want to become a master communicator, you might consider taking some acting or public-speaking lessons: they will provide the techniques and training, and will expose you to exercises where you are required to speak under pressure. Practice makes perfect.

The Not-So-Subtle Steps

So, what messages should you take away from this chapter?

- Before you speak, take a moment to think, 'What I really want to say is ...'
- Get your facts straight and prepare an elevator pitch with three key elements. Remember to ask your listener to confirm what they heard and make sure you establish what happens next and when.
- Ensure the timing of your communication is chosen wisely to get the best response from your audience, and when you speak, speak like a leader.

Research suggests it takes twenty-one days to build or break a habit. Practice these techniques every day for the next three weeks to develop the habit of successful communication.

2

Delivery: Delegation

- *Do you have more work than you can handle?*
- *Do you find your team doesn't always deliver to your high standards?*
- *Do you often find yourself saying, 'I might as well do this myself!'*
- *Are you known as a micromanager?*
- *Do tasks seem to take more of your time the more help you get?*

As much as delegation is about handing duties over to others, it is also about partnering with your team to fulfil the tasks you are given. It works best when everyone agrees on the approach and milestones.

A person's output can be increased by adding energy. The earliest humans harnessed simple tools to improve their productivity. A stone axe brought the task of felling a tree within the capability range of a single person, which would have previously been impossible. Later, pioneers of our species domesticated animals, whose muscle power greatly magnified our own. Later still, natural forces like air and water were put to work, as waterwheels and windmills became the disruptive technologies of their era.

Cornish miners developed steam as a source of power, which allowed them to pump water up from the depths, access lucrative seams of minerals and power the Industrial Revolution. Electricity is the energy of choice today, and cold fusion promises a future of limitless energy, although the timeframe for these developments continues to be vague at best.

This combination of human and natural resources made it possible to transform from primitive hunter–gatherers to the planet's dominant species, capable of almost any physical feat, provided time and ingenuity are in sufficient supply.

However, there is a simpler way of multiplying human capability, one that requires no tools, steam, or nuclear reactions, that is by simply adding more humans. A team working in coordination towards a common goal can achieve what no lone human can. The modern company is a team in many ways. Individuals with specialist skills combine their capabilities to fulfil a shared objective such as the launch and commercialization of a product or service.

Look under the hood of any successful enterprise, and you will see many teams working in concert, outputting a symphony of collaborative mental and physical effort. Team tasks are coordinated by a centralized function comprising the senior management team and chief executive, but often, employees will work autonomously to deliver the specific component they are responsible for within the grand scheme of the operation.

You may also see individuals working in isolation, fulfilling a function so narrow that it is within the capability range of a single person. However, you will rarely see people like this occupying the corner office—no matter how industrious they are. That lofty perch is almost always reserved for those who utilize their skill and experience to set a larger group of people to work, their output far greater than what each individual can achieve alone. In this chapter, we will examine the characteristics and practices that define these people and enable them to bring out the very best in a team.

There are many views on how a leader should best approach the mobilization of their team—from the gently persuasive to the outright dictatorial. There's certainly more than one way to skin this particular cat. Different people respond to different types of stimuli, and leaders gravitate towards approaches that best suit their personality and disposition. Nevertheless, experience shows that some approaches work better than others and, by adopting some basic principles, those who aspire to be leaders can maximize their chances of success.

Let's look at some of those principles.

Respect and Partnership

When given power, it can be tempting to wield it with abandon. After all, what is the point of having a big stick if you don't get to use it? This instinct, seductive as it is, misconceives the nature of authority. Even the most rigorous sergeant major knows that a loud bark and sharp bite are caricatures of the skills they deploy on the parade ground. In the collaborative setting of the corporate office, they're no help at all. Instead, showing respect towards those who report to you and treating them as partners rather than underlings is the key to winning their commitment. Indeed, this is true of most interactions in life.

To cultivate this partnership mentality, consider what your approach would be if you were going to execute a task you want to delegate:

- What is the task intended to achieve?
- Why have you been asked to do it?
- How would you frame it so it makes sense to you?
- What are the key outcomes you are being asked to deliver?
- How would you go about doing it?
- What sort of input would you need to perform the task?
- Who would you consult?
- How much time would you need to get it done to the expected standard?
- Does the workload align with the deadline you have been given?
- And most importantly, how important is this task relative to the others you're currently working on?

Armed with this framework, you can make the best use of your team's time when discussing the task with them. Let's think about how you might do this.

Shared Vision

In the same way you spend time contemplating the task at hand, you should now allow your team to gain their own understanding before having a meeting to agree on the details. This will help them become invested in the task and rally their thoughts before they attend a more detailed discussion. When you finally hold that all-important first meeting, you should make sure you cover and agree on the following:

- The intention or purpose of the task.
- Its importance is relative to other work.
- Its value to the organization.
- The possible approaches to completing the task.
- Key steps that might be taken.

- Expectations on what is to be delivered.
- How you define 'success'.
- A timeline, including specific checkpoints, to monitor progress.

Remember, this is a partnership. It's essential that you ask for and listen to your team member's views and suggestions; it is possible their ideas are better than yours. The key point to remember is that by delegating you are not abdicating responsibility; you are simply sharing responsibility to deliver a collaborative vision.

Right-Size Management

We've established that delegation is a partnership, rather than simply offloading a task to someone else. But how much input should you be having as a manager? Should you provide a rough guideline and step back or dive in and work on the task alongside your team?

These are extremes, so the answer is probably neither. The appropriate degree of engagement will depend on the complexity of the task and how high up it features on your list of priorities. The key variable is the trade-off between getting exactly what you want and supervising so closely that you don't have any bandwidth available for anything else—in which case, you're just another member of the team and need managing yourself!

Finding the right balance usually requires compromise. Sometimes, it's perfectly okay to assign five tasks to five different people in the knowledge that some elements of the output may not be consistent. If these 'look and feel' aspects aren't critical to a successful outcome, this method may be a better use of your resources, rather than striving for perfection and failing to deliver. Although you may have already highlighted your vision of a great result to set a high bar for your team, you should also have an idea of what an acceptable result looks like. It will help you to prioritize and scale your involvement in tasks.

To ensure you're providing the appropriate support while not spreading yourself too thin is to allow your team to complete the task to a point where the core requirements are met but the final fine-tuning is left to the end. You can then incorporate your judgement and expertise to finish the task to the required standard.

As a product development specialist, Alasdair was involved in many projects where the challenge was not so much of generating good ideas as it was marrying them with available resources and the willingness of the company to invest. He found that inspiring team members to work hard and be creative was less of a problem than containing their enthusiasm and keeping them in line with the compromises necessary to get the job done on time and within budget. Product developers are accustomed to an explosion of imagination at the start of a project, followed by the need to rein everything in and impose tight constraints before implementation work begins.

Most developers apply the concept of the minimum viable product (MVP) as an overarching principle. In other words, we know what we would like to do, but what do we absolutely have to do to be commercially successful? It often makes sense to focus on delivering the MVP first and add enhancements later. It is surprising how often the things that so energized people in the early stages of a project no longer look so attractive or vital once the MVP is delivered. Right-size project management isn't just about compromising to ensure efficient use of your time but also about delivering better results.

Allotting Time

Here's a popular rule of thumb for assigning time to different elements of a project. Around 10 to 20 per cent of the available time should be spent together as a team, clearly defining and understanding what it is that needs to be delivered. You should cover the qualitative and quantitative scope, that is, the 'what' and the outline of 'how' you'll deliver it.

Around 70 to 80 per cent should be spent executing the task, gathering data, and developing the product prototype. The leader should have about 10 per cent involvement here, using checkpoints to help steer execution, respond to risks, and troubleshoot.

Around 5 to 10 per cent should be spent fine-tuning the final product. The leader should be heavily involved in this stage to ensure that the quality of what the team is delivering meets the standard that has been set.

Depending on the complexity of the task, a leader should be personally involved in about 30 to 40 per cent of the time allotted to a project. This will allow them to manage multiple tasks and still maintain a healthy balance by entrusting the details to the team.

Harness Peer Support

So far, we've looked at the relationship between a leader and their team and the need for a leader to create a partnership with their team members so the outcome is the best-combined effort of everyone involved, as opposed to an aggregation of individual contributions. As with most things in life, the whole should be greater than the sum of its parts.

Having said that, this particular whole doesn't necessarily need to be limited to the team and its leader. In all business functions, those around you will have a role to play, as well as those above and below you in the corporate pecking order. When it comes to effective collaboration, our peers—and sometimes, our seniors— are also part of our team.

Once again, to get the best out of those around you, respect is key. When you're seeking collaboration with those outside your formal chain of responsibility, explaining and agreeing on the importance of the task to the wider organization becomes even more important. You may need to appeal to those senior to you and maybe even company shareholders. You will need to be able to clearly articulate why a particular initiative deserves firm-wide collaboration and support.

Seeking Help from Peers

Make supportive inquiries when asking for help. After explaining why a project is important, a good leader will often proceed by asking how others in the room will be able to help complete the task. This can be done by simply asking for suggestions or inputs from the team. Any individual in an organization who has a lot of time to spare is probably under-employed, and the company they work for may be struggling to achieve success. Either way, if you've made your case well and your peers see the importance of the project for the company at large, most will be willing to carve out some time to support you.

Offering to have a word with their boss or engaging your own manager to do so on your behalf can help to secure your peers' support and give them the cover they need. Providing assurances that you will minimize disruption to their team—and then sticking to your word—is an important way to show respect for their time.

Keep your peers' commitment low if they don't have any additional resources available, either in terms of budget or time. Your own team will need to carry most of the burden. However, if additional funding is made available, you should feel free to follow the delegation approach we've set out, given that you are 'paying' for your peers' time. In these circumstances, they should be included in review sessions where possible.

Invest in positive alliances on a day-to-day basis so that when the time comes to ask for a favour, the ground is fertile. If the first time you engage a person is to ask for help, it will always be harder to secure their agreement than if you already have a relationship with them—and even better if you've done something for them in the past. We will cover this aspect of professional relationships in Chapter 7, 'Building a Network'.

Real-Life Example: Trade Lifecycle

A few years ago, the financial regulator posed tough questions to the bank where Priyesh was employed. Could it prove that it had a resilient trade management process, covering all transactions from the front office where trades are agreed with clients, to the back office where they are made and recorded? Could it be confident no trades were being lost along the way? Answering these questions required a review of all the dataflow and control processes throughout the entire organization. This was a significant task.

As the manager of a department in the risk management division, it fell to Priyesh to take responsibility for the project. However, it was not a task he could tackle alone or with his team. He needed help from his peers who operated in other parts of the business. To obtain that support, he applied the principles we discussed in this chapter.

He explained the importance of the task, given it was a response to a request from the regulator. If the bank couldn't demonstrate that its processes were satisfactory, it could face hefty fines. By contrast, if it could prove its processes were robust, the regulator might reward the bank by reducing the amount of its regulatory capital—money a bank must hold in reserve to offset risk. A lower capital requirement means more money to invest.

Having established the importance of the task, Priyesh found his peers were more than willing to help, though they were concerned about the burden the project would place on their teams. To mitigate these concerns, Priyesh agreed that his team would coordinate the project to minimize its impact on the other teams.

Priyesh, his team and his peers held a brainstorming exercise to determine the way forward. They zeroed in on a high-level process diagram for each trading area, mapping the key control points, and validating their effectiveness against three criteria—accuracy, completeness and timeliness. Where they uncovered issues, the group would assign a rating of 'amber' or 'red' and identify steps to get them to 'green'.

Priyesh agreed on an approach with his team and peers. They would do the following:

- Map out one trading area first to assess the task and fine-tune their approach.
- Meet at least once a week to monitor their progress.
- Complete their assessment of the first business area within four weeks.
- Create a six-month plan for the wider firm based on what they learnt.

Priyesh was able to secure the resources he needed to cover additional ground, and he forged agreements with his peers regarding the maximum number of hours their teams could free up to provide support. Priyesh and his team managed the overall process but in close coordination with the other teams. He also delivered regular progress reports to the senior management to ensure that each team had adequate cover from their own management chain, and that any competing tasks weren't going to disrupt the project.

This coordinated division of labour across a group of teams working in partnership with senior oversight ensured the project was delivered according to plan. It achieved the desired result, and the benefits were shared by the entire firm—not only the teams involved.

The Not-So-Subtle Steps

Here are some key points to practice and build into your regular management process:

- When the next task lands on your table, consider who in your team can best help you with it. Explain the significance of the task to the selected team members and consult them on how best to approach it.
- Organize a meeting to agree on what will be delivered, including the format, quality expectations and approach, then review the timetable, including any interim deliverables.
- Discuss what external help you might need. Allocate 10 to 20 per cent of your allotted time to this 'thinking and planning' phase before you set it all in motion.
- Allow your team 70 per cent of the overall project time to execute the plan you have agreed on. Hold regular catch-ups to monitor and steer progress.
- Dedicate the remaining 10 per cent to fine-tuning the output and ensuring it meets your particular standards of quality.
- If you need help from peers, ensure there is clear agreement on the project's importance to the firm and agree on the level of resources you will need them to commit. Seek additional resources from the company to facilitate the process if you need to.

Best of luck expanding your impact by forging better partnerships with your team and peers!

3

Delivery: Managing Projects

- *Have you been given a project to manage?*
- *Do you need advice on how to run it smoothly from start to finish?*
- *Are you working on a project that's already turning into a bit of a bumpy ride?*
- *Would you like to ensure you understand what is vital for a project's success?*

There are several key elements upon which every project depends. A successful project manager will take care of this 'pulse', like a good doctor who delivers the correct advice to keep their patients healthy, or a chess master who plays the game by running multiple scenarios to plot the best route to a checkmate. In short, a project is an endeavour to:

- achieve a specific goal
- within an agreed budget and
- within an agreed time frame

If any of these terms are unclear, the project is poorly defined. Without all three specifications in place, it cannot be considered a project at all. There is nothing about this concept that is unusual or unique to business. Whether consciously or not, we continually manage projects in our professional and private lives. No one lives their life following someone else's direction all the time. For example, when we plan a holiday, we assume the role of project manager. We often ask ourselves the following:

- Where do we want to go?
- What do we want to do?
- What is our budget?
  In project-management speak, these are our *key requirements* and *business case.*

- When do we want to go?
- How long will it take us to get there and back?
- How much time will we spend in each location along the way? The *key phases* or *milestones.*

- Whose support do we need to reach our destination? Our *key resources.*

- Who else is going on the trip with us? Our *stakeholders.*

- Is one member of the group paying a greater share of the holiday fees?
  A *key sponsor.*

- If circumstances change, how will we let our travelling companions know?
  Status reporting and *stakeholder expectation* management.

- What do we need to prepare for the holiday? For example, how do we book flights and hotels, arrange airport transfers, and source the appropriate travel documentation?
- How do we handle a situation like running out of time or money?
- What's our schedule? For example, are we allowing ourselves enough time to get to the airport and preparing an itinerary to ensure we make the most of our trip?
  A *project plan* and *critical path*.

- How was our holiday? On returning we can leave a review of our experience on a travel website so that others can learn from us.
  A *post-implementation review*.

Sounds simple? It can be if we consider all dimensions of a project carefully. Project management is mostly common sense, but certain elements of a project are more important than others. A good project manager teases these vital elements out, watches them like a hawk, and plays the project like a chess master, staying several steps ahead of the game.

The Project Formula

There are several different methodologies that project managers swear by like Waterfall, Agile, and PRINCE2. Each one has its merits depending on the task at hand, but regardless of the model you choose, we recommend observing a five-key-step project formula:

1. Inception: What is the need, benefit and cost—and for whom? What criteria will determine the success of the project?

2. Design: What are the key requirements—the 'must-haves' and the 'nice-to-haves'? What is the broad solution to meeting these needs?

3. Approach: How will you deliver the solution? What's your plan? What are the key steps? Whose support will you need to carry them out?

4. Delivery: How would you execute your tasks while keeping a close eye on progress and achieving your goal?

5. Post-delivery: How would you learn from the experience so you can achieve as much—or more—next time? What follow-up steps should you take now that the project is complete?

Cast your eye back over the holiday-planning example above, and you will see that we follow a very similar formula when making personal arrangements. Next, we will look at each step in more depth and the 'Black Art' techniques that experienced leaders use.

Black Art: The Project Story

The best project managers have a clear picture of how they will deliver a project from start to finish, almost like a sixth sense. They can recount this as a journey or story to their team and stakeholders. They know where the risks lie, where they can apply pressure, and where there is room to manoeuvre.

If you're not yet able to summarize the end-to-end journey of your project plan—including the key risks—you need to spend time mastering this and keeping it in mind.

Step 1: Inception—The Business Case

Every project needs a business case—a summary of why the goal is worth the effort required to achieve it. When appealing for support, your business case is what will persuade those around you to invest in your project. If you are handed a task by your boss, you will want to see or develop a clear business case to understand what makes the project worthwhile and achievable. If there is no clear business case, you should probably push back. There is no value in embarking on a journey with no clear destination.

Alasdair was asked to deliver a new product that would help drinks manufacturers understand which spirits and cocktails were 'hot' in different markets around the world. It soon became clear that the proposed methodology—forming a network of bar staff who could report on drinking trends in real time—wasn't achievable within a budget that would deliver a profit, so the project was shelved before it could even get started.

With great effort, the product could have been delivered but not at a cost that would have allowed it to enjoy commercial success. The business case did not hold up, so scrapping it and dedicating that time to something else was the right thing to do. The business case or project charter must cover three core issues:

1. Why are we doing this? What do we stand to gain from it?
2. What are the tangible benefits of the project and for whom?
3. How will we measure our success and demonstrate it to others?

This 'success test' needs to be as concrete as possible. We might define success in terms of an increase in sales by a specific percentage or penetration into a new market. It needs to be articulated clearly in business terms but also in a way that makes an accountable difference to the business, its customers' lives, and ultimately, its bottom line. You should endeavour to answer the following questions:

- What benefit will emerge from this project?
- What harm could we cause by not doing it?

- What resources will we need in terms of people, systems and services?
- What costs will we incur and who are we expecting to pay?
- Who will reap the rewards of the project, and when?
- What are we committing to deliver and what are we explicitly excluding?
- What risks are associated with the project and how can they be mitigated?
- Can we articulate our approach in a way that reassures others of its feasibility?
- Who will be expected to sign off and approve the business case?
- Are there key success criteria that can be measured quantitatively or qualitatively—for example, this project will save x amount of money?

Black Art: Early Risk Framing

It is impossible to eliminate risk, but a systematic approach can minimize it. To frame a project properly, potential risks should be anticipated at the outset. An effective project leader will lay out all the risks clearly, managing both the scope of the project and the expectations of stakeholders.

The old project management adage of 'under-promise and over-deliver' is a simplification that makes stakeholders feel cheated, but it also contains an important lesson. From the beginning, an experienced project leader will clarify a range of possible outcomes based on any variables they've identified and will use these exchanges to gauge their stakeholders' appetite for risk. That means specifying the following:

- What is the minimum that the project must deliver?
- Which outcomes would stakeholders prioritize beyond that minimum?

- What are the 'stretch targets', that is, not critical to success but can be pursued by the team if circumstances allow?

The key is to 'take risks transparently' in a way that is agreeable to all stakeholders. Sometimes, the value of a prize means it's worth 'shooting for the stars', and if you pull it off, you could be considered a star in your own right. However, should you shoot and miss, you want guarantees that the organization will rally around. That means ensuring everyone is aware of what could go wrong, and if it does, how they'll contribute to fixing the problem.

In short, the more you think the project through beforehand, the more in control you will be and the less likely you will be taken by surprise down the road.

Here's an example.

Priyesh was once asked to deliver a project that had considerable upsides for the bank but represented a major change to the way the organization calculated risk. It required a lot of work and needed to be delivered in an extremely ambitious twelve-month period. From the outset, Priyesh knew there simply weren't enough hours in the day to complete such a huge task.

He made the senior stakeholders aware of the problem but also offered a solution. He suggested extending the working day from twelve hours a day to nearly thirty by taking advantage of time-zone differences by mobilizing teams in New York, London and Singapore. Nevertheless, it was still risky, particularly now that it involved coordinating a global team.

With juicy rewards dangling in front of their faces like a carrot on a stick, the stakeholders gave Priyesh the green light to proceed and guaranteed their support in the event the project

> ran into difficulties. Priyesh, his team, and the stakeholders
> brought the project back from the brink and to fruition together,
> with the team receiving significant plaudits for their efforts in
> supporting the firm's business plan.

Step 2: Design—Key Requirements

If the business case establishes the project on solid ground, setting
out the key requirements in detail ensures it stays there.

This is where you spell out your minimum, highly desirable,
and stretch target requirements in detail. You should not only spell
out 'what' needs to be delivered down to the most granular level of
detail possible, but also the 'why'—so the team can understand the
spirit of the desired outcome when they consider how they're going
to deliver the project.

At this stage, you are not yet engaging with the 'how' part of the
project—or at least, not in any great detail. We want to avoid closing
off options by specifying too narrowly how the project should be
implemented. For each desired outcome, you should gather:

- Key inputs—data or triggers
- Processing required—exact calculations or workflow steps
- Key outputs—the end product
- Non-functional requirements—for example, response or
  turnaround times
- Any specific 'look-and-feel' requirements
- What's not required

The most effective way to understand what needs to be done is to
consider how the output will work from the client's point of view—
the user experience.

In a world of machines, mathematics, models and processes, we sometimes lose sight of who we are creating the project for—human beings. A powerful technique you can use to gather requirements is to role-play scenarios. For example, if we are creating a project to deliver a website, first consider:

- Who will be visiting the site?
- What kind of experience do they want?
- What would they find useful or interesting?
- Where can we get this information from?
- How can we make it easily digestible?
- How do we want the client to spend their time?
- Will they want interaction—a chat session, for example?
- How would they typically want to end the experience?
- What would they take away from it?

It doesn't have to be an exercise of the imagination. If you can find a representative user and role-play scenarios with them using the product, you can really bring it all to life.

Black Art: Put Client Experience First

Role-playing use cases help you develop a better understanding of different events that can shape the use of your proposed product or service. To take this a step further, you can use some black magic to define the deliverable in relation to the client experience.

Don't tie yourself or your stakeholders to a solution too early. Instead, brainstorm innovative ideas and look at options by analysing the market. What are your competitors doing—even in other markets with similar customer relationships?

Spend time with your clients and stakeholders and watch how they work. Does the problem you are aiming to solve actually exist? And does it take the form you have hypothesized in your business plan? For example, there's no point in designing an innovative magnetic pen holder if nobody is using pens anymore!

Work through how you can improve someone's life with what you're aiming to deliver, without committing to a detailed solution. Let the detail emerge from your observation of their needs. It could be that not everything you have proposed in your brainstorming sessions is possible, but at least you have pushed the boundaries of your imagination and increased the odds of producing something that you can develop into a conceivable option.

Priyesh recalls designing a unique and complex risk management dashboard for a bank. He involved the most knowledgeable, senior risk managers to help him establish the project's requirements, repeatedly brainstorming possible designs to ensure his team was presenting what stakeholders wanted to see. At this stage, the technical plumbing wasn't high up on the agenda, to not stifle the team's ideas.

This process allowed the team to visualize a key output that would look great and be useful. It may sound risky, but Priyesh and his team found it liberating, and the result won several awards. Furthermore, everyone involved in the project felt excited and energized by it, developing a real sense of ownership over the end product.

However, there is always a need for a strict reality check before a project advances too far; the art is in dreaming a little first before coming down to earth! All too often, technical norms dominate processes and limit the project to mediocrity before more imaginative and innovative solutions have a chance. It is important to make it clear that you will have to be more practical down the line. Manage expectations so everyone can get their ideas down on the table while understanding that they may not make the final cut.

To summarize, innovative leaders allow imaginations to run free. They consider all the ideas available to them in the early stages and encourage maximum creativity before taking a hard look at what is practical and deliverable within the project's constraints. Think about it, if Steve Jobs had been a practical man, we might never have seen the smartphone!

Step 3: Approach—Who Does What?

A project is a collection of coordinated tasks that fit together to produce an outcome. In practice, this means people doing different things following a collaborative design.

Think of an Airbus A380 airliner—the wings may be assembled in Wales, the body in France, and the tail in Germany. Imagine all these parts being brought together for final assembly, only to find the wings are too long for the body, which was too narrow for the tail—not a recipe for a successful, fifty-billion-dollar aircraft manufacturing business!

Assigning tasks within a project is a critical steps for two reasons. First, each task requires its own skillset, and you will want to be sure that each team member is working in their most effective position. Second, someone must be accountable for each separate element of the project. Accountability means being responsible for ensuring an element progresses in line with the overall plan, keeping the project manager up to speed on how things are going and carrying the can when things go wrong.

Here, it is worth taking a systematic approach to this essential element of the project plan. Identify the key roles first, then map the right people to those roles.

- Who is essential to shape the business concept?
- Who is best equipped to provide technical direction?
- Who has the skills to do the work?
- Who can ensure it all comes together?
- Who will ultimately benefit from the product?

You should also set out how much time each of the various roles is likely to take up. You may call on some people to support the project alongside their main roles. For this, you need to be clear, specific and upfront about time commitments.

Once you have specified the different roles, it is time to think about who the best people might be for each job. You should also ask whether others can provide support or substitute if your first choice is not available. Identify your first, second and third choices. You may even want to hire a fresh face or transfer someone to your team.

You should also be clear about who needs to be kept in the loop on how the project is progressing, even if they are not getting their hands dirty. They may be paying the bills, or they might just be an interested party close to the initiative.

There are many tools, frameworks and applications to help with this, but we recommend the RACI matrix. It will help you identify the correct person for each key role in the project and define the time commitment they require. The RACI matrix distinguishes between four roles:

Responsible—those who do the work
Accountable—where the buck stops
Consulted—providing advice and guidance
Informed— not involved but kept up to speed

Next, think about delivering a pricing calculation:

- Mr Jones is *responsible* for producing the calculation within two to three weeks.
- He reports to Mrs Plum who, as the head accountant, is *accountable*.
- He will *consult* Mrs Patel, taking one or two days out of the overall project timeline.
- He will *inform* Mr Yu how the project is going at weekly fifteen-minute meetings.

As you will have gathered by now, delivering a project is much more than simply doing the work. Your project may involve numerous people in different departments and locations, working overlapping schedules. Governance is key to keeping this complicated show on the road. You need to be crystal clear about who has the responsibility to review, own and provide oversight for the delivery of a project.

Ensure the right people remain committed to the project throughout by setting up an appropriate governance meeting and reporting schedule. Then, form a steering committee that meets regularly to review progress and take tough decisions to ensure the project stays on target. For larger programmes, create several smaller working groups to be responsible for different aspects of the project, reporting to an overarching steering committee.

You will also need to clearly define the flow of information between the two tiers. For example, the steering committee may be responsible for defining direction, deliverables, budgets and investigations for the working groups. Each working group will report progress, exceptions and proposals to the steering committee.

Black Art: The Visionary and the Executor

Let's look at two key roles that can greatly increase a project's chances of success. The first is the business sponsor—a visionary, empowered to make decisions and tailor the scope of the project to ensure success. The second is the project leader, an exceptional executor who dares to push back against the sponsor in cases where their specialized knowledge may enable them to make better and more informed decisions.

If you are one of these people, you have a considerable burden of responsibility for your team and organization. If you don't fill at least one of these key roles—either yourself or by drafting in a talented colleague—your project will probably be harder to deliver.

Being a top-class business sponsor doesn't come naturally to everyone. You need to be able to conceive a vision and know when to compromise in the face of practical constraints—and when not to. There are many notable examples of great sponsors and visionaries, including Steve Jobs and Bill Gates. You may know someone similar in your organization.

As a sponsor, you need to be clear on what will deliver the intent of the project. You need to go beyond a technical blueprint to a deeper understanding of what the project is truly designed to achieve. The visionary sponsor knows when to shoot for the stars and when to pull back, managing other stakeholders to ensure continued progress. They know which battles to fight and which to concede in order to win the war. A pragmatic, knowledgeable, and savvy sponsor can lead a project to success without delivering everything.

On the flip side, a less experienced business sponsor can either demand too little, not deliver enough value or deliver too much, stretching the delivery team beyond its capabilities. There are three key aspects to being a great sponsor:

1. Decision making: Take decisions that move a project forward towards your vision.
2. Engagement: Be involved enough so you can intervene in time if necessary.
3. Compromise: What should you compromise on to get the project over the line?

A project manager holds the sponsor's vision close to their heart. It's a highly privileged position and requires a strong desire to make a difference. They must be completely aligned with the sponsor, but they aren't just a 'yes' person. Rather, they are a trusted adviser who drives the vision forward but also proposes alternatives when risks begin to build.

A project manager must be courageous enough to take measured risks. Delivering a high-quality output usually takes a project manager who can push the status quo with enough tenacity to keep their team engaged until the most optimal solutions are found.

Priyesh recalls situations where, as project manager, he has worked through the night, tracing code with IT developers to ensure the solution works. Of course, it was the experienced IT developers who ultimately found the solution, but setting that tone of 'going the extra mile' is down to the project manager. It is by employing this mindset that Priyesh delivered several near-impossible projects throughout his career.

Sometimes, the project manager needs to know when to compromise. Priyesh recalls a project where the coding for a large-scale number-crunching machine was delayed. A key sponsor suggested the team use a spreadsheet solution created by one of the junior analysts, and Priyesh agreed this was what it was going to take to get the project over the line. It wasn't a long-term solution, but it would produce numbers for analysis, buying the project some time while the rest of the team caught up. With this compromise, the team was ultimately able to deliver the project successfully.

Step 4: Delivery—Making It Happen

A detailed project plan will include:

- All the key steps to achieving the goal(s) in order of execution.
- Who is going to do what—and by when?
- Timeframe estimates, with some room for error as a contingency.

Let's ask a couple of fundamental questions using the classic project management triangle commonly known as the Triple Constraint, which takes into consideration resources, scope and time.

- By adding resources, can we deliver faster?
- By reducing the scope, can we deliver faster?

These questions allow good project managers to identify their options, as well as help stakeholders decide what outcomes are delivered, by when and at what cost.

The next step is to assemble the plan, clearly outlining every task and resource, preferably using a professional project management tool like Microsoft Project. Doing so allows you to:

- Balance resources so team members aren't overloaded.
- Run various scenarios to see if you can mitigate risk or finish sooner.

- Agree on the plan with stakeholders, keep it up-to-date, and report progress.

When the time comes to make it happen, be sure to manage the project closely, tracking every step. Guide the ship and let everyone know what's going on so you can manage expectations and be completely transparent throughout.

Black Art: Finger on the Pulse

Professional tools help organize and monitor tasks. However, the real art of project management is tracking its heartbeat or 'pulse', also known as the critical path—the shortest distance from the beginning to the end of the project, containing all the essential elements to deliver it.

Though every project will have a few 'nice-to-have' requirements, a great project manager will try to keep them off the critical path. Once you understand the critical path, you can share it with all the stakeholders and project team, ensuring everyone is on the same page and is able to raise a red flag if anything diverges from the plan.

So, what should be included on a critical path and how do you manage it? Most project management tools can provide an indication of what a critical path is, but the real questions we are trying to answer are as follows:

- What is the minimum scope?
- What is the bare minimum we need to do to deliver it?
- What are the key dependencies between the tasks?
- In what order must they be executed?
- Can we do certain tasks quicker or in parallel to shorten the critical path?

Once all this has been assessed, you can map the project's critical path on a simple Gantt chart and walk all your stakeholders and team members through it.

You should track the project's journey along the critical path almost robotically, keeping your finger on the pulse at all times. That way, if there is any risk of delay—or an opportunity to shorten the critical path—you can intervene in good time.

Black Art: Mitigating Risk

Once you've identified a critical path, it becomes your path to success. Anything that endangers the critical path needs to be carefully identified and managed. Assessing the risks to a project following the critical path provides a tangible focus for a successful project leader. It allows risk mitigation efforts to focus on what's most important first, which is clearing the path forward.

We have delivered many successful, large-scale programmes by focusing on these two elements—the critical path and related risk mitigation strategies. Making changes to a project once it's begun is a key risk. Agility is important; after all, it's rare that we fully understand what we need from the very start. However, we need to be disciplined and acknowledge the impact that shifting the goalposts can have on a project in motion.

It's fine to accept changes that don't affect the critical path, especially if it helps to keep sponsors happy, but where these choices endanger the critical path, the project manager should become a close adviser to the sponsor and push back if necessary. Sometimes, a project manager needs to make difficult decisions to ensure the project's success.

Priyesh recalls a major programme where, having reviewed and recorded several risks, he informed key sponsors that it was highly likely the project would fail if the team didn't control additions to the scope that put the critical path at risk. For example, the organization's finance department had requested nearly a hundred different reports to support a new trading business. Meeting these requirements was nigh-on impossible given the short timeframe, irrespective of how many resources were being thrown at the project. As Priyesh brought these risks to everyone's attention, demonstrating how all scenarios led to a high risk of failure, the heads of the business agreed they could make do with twenty key reports in the first phase, contributing to the project's success while maintaining essential deliverables.

If it isn't possible to delay a change that affects the critical path, reworking the plan and ensuring everyone is aware of the new baseline is essential to maintain a proper connection between project teams, leaders and stakeholders.

So, to manage risks and ensure the success of your project:

- List all risks and issues that could affect—or are affecting— the project.
- Prioritize risks that may impact the critical path.
- Track and mitigate risks regularly, every day if possible.
- Ensure the project team and stakeholders are fully engaged in risk management.

Manage changes with a risk-based approach, being more flexible around decisions that don't affect the critical path. Then, adjust the project plan and manage expectations accordingly. Proactive risk management, proper communication of changing risk profiles, and adjusting the project plan to reflect any agreed changes enable an accomplished project leader to keep everyone involved fully up to speed.

Step 5: Post-Delivery—Live to Fight Another Day

Getting a project over the line equals success. Making a difference by following the critical path while taking pragmatic, risk-measured calls when adjusting the scope allows a project to deliver value. Earlier, we illustrated how joint risk management between sponsors, the visionary and the executor often provides the best outcome.

The route to the finish line could be close to the original project plan, or it might reflect substantial changes that were incorporated along the way. As long as all agree that there is value to be had for the organization, the project should go live and be successful. Then the team can celebrate its achievement and recuperate before regrouping to deliver the next phase.

A great project leader knows when they have enough to go live and what they need to prioritize in future phases. Going back to Priyesh's project, after the finance department's request for a hundred reports had been reduced to twenty, he agreed to add another twenty in the next phase to improve the department's efficiency. As a result, he was able to deliver the first phase on time and maintain the finance department's trust by meeting its needs.

Finally, when all is done, take some time with your team to look at:

- What went well
- What can be improved next time
- Priorities for the next phase

This type of analysis provides a practical, post-implementation review for a growing organization. It's not a witch hunt but simply a factual learning experience where issues and solutions can be highlighted without worrying about who was responsible. The only exception is where confusion around roles caused issues, but even in this situation, the discussion should be totally depersonalized, referring to roles rather than individuals.

The Not-So-Subtle Steps

Let's recap the key steps of running a successful project.

- Start in the right frame of mind by awakening your inner project manager, positively brimming with a desire to do something worthwhile.
- Structure your project using the key phases of inception, design, approach, delivery and post-delivery, with an aim to build a clear story in your mind.
- Ensure you formulate a business case that focuses on key priorities, differentiating the minimum requirements from the 'nice-to-haves', outlining your approach and managing stakeholders' expectations regarding key risks.
- Use role-play to bring project requirements to life. Partner design and technical experts with real end-users. Actively prompt participants to let their imaginations run free so you can discover what they really want and what will deliver real value to them. Incorporate the practicalities later to create a pragmatic solution.
- Don't underestimate the importance of clarifying roles and responsibilities. Who needs to do what? How much time do we need from them? The two key roles of 'visionary sponsor' and 'courageous executor' must work in close partnership.
- Organize tasks and resources by running scenarios that flex the project triangle—resources, scope and time. Identify the critical path and make the project plan transparent for

all to see. Keep your finger on the pulse. Maintain a strict change-control discipline but allow the flexibility to add additional, non-critical-path items to help you deliver the most value with the lowest possible risk.

- Identify, discuss and mitigate risks, especially relating to tasks on the critical path. Perhaps compromise by delaying something non-essential until a future phase.

- Learn lessons from the project so you can do better next time, but don't make it personal. Focus on the what and how rather than the who.

Best of luck delivering more successful projects. Remember, every project is different, so it's always good to be adaptable, as long as you have all the critical elements in place.

4

Controlling Your Emotions

- *Do you find yourself becoming stressed at work or in your daily life?*
- *Do you sometimes feel like you overreact in certain situations?*
- *Would you like to have more control over your emotions?*
- *Do you want to be more proactive and use pressure to your advantage?*

Pressure can be an effective tool if channelled well. If we have a proper awareness of how we respond emotionally to challenging circumstances, we can use that knowledge to pursue a business solution and benefit our personal situation. This is one of the crucial abilities that define a successful leader.

British politician David Willets is affectionately known as 'Two Brains', presumably a reference to his intelligence. However, the nickname didn't serve him well. Allies were put off by it and opponents derided it. Willets is fully deserving of the name, but then, aren't we all? Every human has two brains. One is the primal organ we inherited from our ancestors; the other is gifted to us throughout the course of evolution as a species. That's the swollen, crinkly part at the top, medically referred to as the cerebral cortex.

Of course, this is a criminal simplification, but the underlying point is important. We react to experiences twice. Our first reaction is an unconscious reflex from the lower brain, physically translated via a sudden flush of hormones that prime our muscles for action. The second is a slower, more considered evaluation from our upper brain, deploying human skills such as empathy, imagination and logical reasoning. The first is tuned to keep us safe in a hostile natural environment; the second, to leverage our competitive intellectual advantage over other species to exploit whatever situation we find ourselves in.

The impact of this two-track processing system on human behaviour was explored in depth by two Israeli psychologists, Daniel Kahneman and Amos Tversky.[1] Their findings have become the basis for a new school of social sciences and economics that examines human decision-making. For our purposes, the interesting part of this research explores how our two brains interact in stressful situations. The problem is, while our lower brain has our best interests at heart, the way it responds is often inappropriate within complex social situations. However, because the lower brain gets first dibs on determining our reaction, by the time the upper brain catches up, it is often too late.

Throw in the effects of our own nature and styles of behaviour, and you have a complex system that responds to stressful situations in unpredictable ways. In the animal kingdom, responses fall broadly into two categories: fight or flight. Confront the situation head-on, or retreat and find another solution.

1   Kahneman, D. (2011). *Thinking, fast and slow*. New York: Farrar, Straus and Giroux.

There is however a third response that some animals adopt when the first two options aren't appropriate, and that is to freeze. For some creatures, this state of paralysis is a well-adapted defence mechanism, confusing an attacker or allowing the creature to camouflage itself. For others, it is nothing more than psychic collapse. Overwhelmed by stress, the body goes into preservation mode and the decision-making capability is suspended. In business, it's easy to become overwhelmed in situations where the pressure is so intense that you can't move forwards or backwards. Such moments can be fatal for a high-flying career.

Alasdair remembers being invited to a meeting with his CEO to deliver an update on a product in which the company saw great promise. Alasdair was halfway through a wordy presentation when the CEO interrupted: 'Tell me in two sentences what this product is *for*.'

Unfortunately, Alasdair hadn't read this book and so, he was unversed in the art of the elevator pitch. He froze for what felt like an eternity. The CEO leant forward, then sat back and sighed. Thankfully, Alasdair's immediate boss was also present and rescued the situation by coming up with a synopsis of the idea. The meeting continued to a relatively satisfactory conclusion, but Alasdair's reputation—and ego—had been singed.

In today's corporate work environment, pressure is almost a way of life. Some of the most important business decisions—those that have the greatest impact on projects, organizations and individual careers—are made when pressure is at its highest.

The most effective leaders have learnt to manage pressure, utilize it when it's warranted, and diffuse it when it isn't. All the while, our impatient lower brain is rushing us into premature action. Pulling this off takes self-awareness and attentiveness to situations, coupled with an understanding of how to manage ourselves and our teams.

This is a vast topic and one that has produced acres of research. We will concentrate on some simple yet powerful methods. These are techniques that some of the most accomplished leaders have used to manage themselves and the pressure cookers they operate in.

Know Thyself

The key to all this is awareness, that is, knowing what makes us tick, given our human nature, evolution and upbringing. Awareness allows us to understand ourselves, reprogramme our brains, and redirect our behaviour. In many respects, our habitual behaviours play second fiddle to our responses, but it is reasonable to assume that most of us would prefer the way we react to be more thoughtful and consistent.

Research has taught us that we cannot control our fight or flight response, which happens at a subconscious or neurological level before our conscious mind can consider the options.

However, we can:

- Become aware of our trigger situations and prepare for them.
- Notice reactions as they emerge so we can deal with them accordingly.
- Reduce stress by creating an environment that promotes positivity.
- Potentially learn to prevent these responses altogether.

The fight or flight response is so fundamental to human nature that it is challenging to alter. However, through awareness, intent and practice, we can make a tangible difference in how we respond to stress—to the benefit of ourselves and the people around us. Let's look at a couple of real-life situations to help us understand and shape our reactions better.

You're walking in the park, minding your own business, and enjoying the fresh air and sunshine. Suddenly, a jogger runs into you from behind, almost knocking you over. They carry on running without so much as glancing backwards. Your immediate reaction is probably one of shock, then anger. How inconsiderate of them! Then they fall to the ground and start shaking. As you approach them, you can tell they're having an epileptic seizure.

What do you think happens to your anger and resentment at this moment? Most of us would empathize immediately, now that we have a better understanding of the situation. We would do whatever possible to help, and even seek medical help if needed.

This emotional roller coaster demonstrates how our fight or flight reaction takes immediate effect, but once logic and understanding come into play, we gain perspective. The challenge, of course, is that we may have said some offensive things to that individual before logical analysis had a chance to take over.

This is an extreme example, but we can be faced with such analogous situations every day of our lives. While we cannot fully control our fight or flight reaction, it helps if we become aware of it and learn to let it pass without causing us problems. Once we do that, we can also choose to walk away, cursing in our minds rather than out loud, or try to observe the unfolding situation as if we were on the outside looking in.

Try bringing your conscious mind into play by saying to yourself, 'Ah, here we go, I can feel my emotions taking over. Let's give this some time to settle before responding.' This split-second observation and consequential shift in perspective allow our upper brain to take the upper hand. We can use this time to gather more information and respond in a more informed manner.

Confronted by a situation like the one we described above, the experienced leader may have been able to minimize any immediate overreaction. It is unlikely they would be able to fully suppress their emotional reaction, possibly letting slip a cursory, 'Hey, watch out!'

Unaware of the reason for the other person's actions, the leader might give them the benefit of the doubt too. As their natural, emotional reaction subsides, their upper brain regains control, warning them not to blow things out of proportion. Ultimately, they would maintain their composure, even if there was no good reason for the other person's actions.

While we cannot control our environment and the variables within it, we are responsible for how we react to them. The most effective leaders keep this awareness at the forefront and only allow their fighting instinct to kick in after a period of conscious reasoning.

Let's try another example.

You attend a meeting with your manager regarding an assignment you've been working on for the past few days. As you start presenting the results, you notice your manager seems displeased and looks as though he's reacting negatively to some of your findings.

Immediately, you're uncomfortable, overcome with worry, and feeling rejected. You start trying to explain the project in more detail, but to no avail. You begin to get upset and flustered. Your subconscious takes you to a place where you think your boss is judging you, perhaps even thinking of replacing you. You feel at risk—your livelihood threatened, your confidence shaken, and your sense of self undermined.

Not letting your imagination run away with you is key here. Before your lower brain seizes control, recognize that you're beginning a downward spiral. Always think, 'Ah, here we go, I can feel my emotions taking over.' This will shift you into a third-person perspective and help you to depersonalize the situation.

Next, ask your manager a logical question: 'You don't seem too keen. Is there something concerning you?' The issue may be a simple misunderstanding or a small error. Seeking guidance and making a commitment to return in a timely manner might win you a second opportunity.

It could be that your manager has their own personal issue. Perhaps they've fought with their partner, or their child is unwell. It could be some other matter, unrelated to your meeting. If that's the case, you had been fretting over nothing!

As in the previous example, getting the facts straight before jumping to conclusions is critical, and keeping a cool head until this happens will help reduce the build-up of stress. Assumptions can be a dangerous health hazard.

Awareness-and-Control Formula

Building on these examples, we can construct a framework for controlling situations.

Be aware of situations that trigger your fight or flight reaction. Anticipate them or avoid them altogether. Note when a situation has triggered a negative reaction in you so you can maintain or regain control. Better still, if you can identify the kind of situations that push your buttons, you can learn to manage them better.

Identify your core triggers. Perhaps you're scrupulously honest and are triggered by people trying to deceive you—or even bending the truth slightly. It could be that you need job security for your family, and anything that threatens that immediately puts you on your guard.

Understanding your core triggers helps you anticipate when a dangerous situation is arising and gives you an opportunity to prepare yourself.

Notice the reaction emerging so you can deal with it and reduce collateral damage. Give yourself time to look at the situation as a third party, using your upper-brain mantra: 'Ah, here we go, I can feel my emotions taking over. Let's give this some time to settle before responding.' Depersonalize the situation and buy time for your logical brain to seek and process the facts. It's almost like emulating an out-of-body experience. With a little practice, this incredibly powerful tool will help you regain control.

Next, consider if the situation is worth escalating. A powerful technique employed by leaders is to ask the question: 'What is the upside and downside of reacting to this?' A quick analysis can give you a clearer perspective and stop you from rushing into a reaction that may go against you in the long term.

The amount of stress we feel depends to a degree on the atmosphere our superiors create for us. We all contribute to the work environment for ourselves and those around us, but the best leaders take ownership of the well-being of their team.

The most successful leaders we've worked with create a pleasurable, somewhat relaxed, and maybe even a fun environment to work in. They ensure people clearly understand why their work is important, worthwhile and special. People working in such environments cope better with deadlines and are less likely to become overwhelmed. They approach challenges with enthusiasm and passion, rather than fear.

Given we spend most of our lives at work, we should be able to share some joy. We need to maintain a balanced perspective of what's important and what we can probably manage without. That way, we can prevent piling the pressure on ourselves and our colleagues.

That's not to say we can compromise on key priorities, but we should make a rigorous effort to prioritize what matters versus what's 'nice to have'. A successful leader helps their team keep things in perspective, maybe even taking some personal risk to make the environment sustainable for the team, despite multiple requests from various stakeholders.

Where a leader sees pressure building, they should provide some breathing space. It could be something as simple as ordering in dinner for late workers, sending people home early after a tough assignment, or even renegotiating the deliverable if possible.

Successful leaders notice a negative shift in the atmosphere at work and engage to redirect or reframe the situation. They may compromise where they didn't intend to if they see a chance to defuse a situation, providing direction that may not answer all the questions but might be good enough to move the team forward.

Finally, celebrating the team's successes and rewarding people through praise and positive reinforcement can act as a pressure-release valve and a powerful motivator.

The Not-So-Subtle Steps

Start practising these steps to gain emotional control:

- Lighten the mood by creating an environment that promotes positivity and productivity. Ensure work is prioritized, contributions are recognized, and pressure valves are released in a timely manner whenever tension starts to build.
- Write down the triggers that kick-start your emotional reactions. Notice when a situation is likely to generate a negative emotional response and shift your awareness by looking at it from an outsider's perspective. Let your upper brain buy time for you to calm down and your logical brain kick in.
- Finally, keep things in perspective. Judge how much you should invest in a situation based on the potential return. There's no point expending time and energy for next to no reason. 'Life's too short,' as they say, so ration your emotional energies.

These lessons require focus and practice. It will take several weeks to change your behaviour and responses, if not longer.

However, even raising your level of awareness and taking baby steps to provide more measured responses will yield significant benefits, both in your work and personal life. Best of luck gaining greater control over your emotional state.

5

Managing Your Time

- *Do you sometimes feel time is running away from you?*
- *Do you find there just aren't enough hours in the day?*
- *Is there hardly any 'life' in your work–life balance?*
- *Do you have difficulty 'switching off?'*
- *Would you like to achieve more with the time you have?*

Imagine you're a military leader with 86,400 troops at your command. That's a lot of soldiers, but you still need strategic nous to be truly formidable. Your success depends not only on the size of your army but also on how you choose to deploy each of your troops.

You wouldn't send foot soldiers to fight the cavalry. You wouldn't use riflemen for close-quarters combat. You wouldn't leave the bulk of your force relaxing in the barracks while a vanguard took on the opposing force alone. If you master the skill of dedicating the right troops to the right task at the right time, you will be equal to the most exacting military challenge, and it would take a bold adversary to challenge you!

Planning how to use your time is much the same. There are 86,400 seconds in a day. That's 86,400 soldiers at your command—a powerful force indeed. But the key to your success is in how you use each of those soldiers. In other words, how you manage your time.

Core Warrior Principle

Remember when you were at school and had a structured timetable? Double maths, gym, English, lunch, music, double science, cricket and home.

Our time was not our own, but we knew we were in good hands. After all, the curriculum was designed to give us enough time to learn so we could pass our exams. Of course, it got more difficult when we had to organize ourselves to revise or do homework.

Every student finds their own rhythm. Some work in the morning, some at night; some in the library, others in the park. Most would have worked out how much time they had and how much they would need to prepare for their exams, and then organized themselves accordingly.

When we leave school and kick off our careers, we have to find our own way, empowered to organize most of our time ourselves. As Uncle Ben Parker said to Spiderman, 'With great power, comes great responsibility.' Not the most traditional source of inspirational professional advice perhaps, but the message here is extremely powerful. Time is a precious commodity. It represents both opportunity and opportunity cost. With every minute of our day, we are either making a time investment or paying a time tax.

Take a moment now to think about how you divide up your typical working day. There is no right or wrong way to spend your time, but most successful leaders have identified and achieved a balance that's right for them.

The core principle of warrior time management is figuring out:

- What balance is right for you?
- How much time do you need to commit in the short term to win the battle?
- How much time do you need to commit in the long term to win the war?

Have you ever heard of generals and commanders running into battle without planning their attack, regularly reviewing their progress, and adapting their tactics accordingly? Absolutely not. To apply the core warrior principle of time management to your own life, spend a few minutes in your 'war room' engaging in a few essential exercises.

Make Time to Prioritize Critical Tasks Early on

Start by taking fifteen to thirty minutes to plan how you're going to approach the day's key tasks. Priyesh prefers to spend his journey to work prioritizing the two or three key activities he needs to focus on during that day. Once he reaches office, he spends another fifteen to twenty minutes planning, preparing, prioritizing and deciding whose help he'll seek.

Book Time for Additional Strategizing

A senior MD and board member says you should take at least an hour a day to focus on contemplating and working towards longer term goals. It may not always be possible—or necessary—but blocking thirty minutes each day out of your diary gives you an opportunity to be more proactive and effective.

'Time-Box' Your Tasks and Create Bursts of Achievements

You need to do your work and do it well, so make time for it. Most people find they work better in short bursts. Perhaps break your diary up into thirty-minute slots that allow for twenty minutes of focused work followed by a ten-minute break.

Although you should focus on a task without interruption, this way, you leave a little room for unavoidable intrusions. A commitment to do something for a short period can help get through tasks, as our brains generally can't focus on anything for longer than twenty minutes.

Whatever you do, try to reach some sort of milestone so you can give yourself a pat on the back for having achieved something. You can always review your work and refine it during the next time slot, but try to get as near as possible to a completed unit before you pause.

Breaking up tasks and showing progress at the same time is an art but very satisfying if you can master it. Think of it as a mini 'SMART' objective:

Specific
Measurable
Achievable
Realistic
Time-Boxed

For example, if you're writing a paper, essay or slide presentation:

- You could spend your first twenty-minute burst writing the core contents or titles of each section and preparing the outline. You will have achieved a logical structure for the story you want to tell—a great use of twenty minutes.

- After a ten-minute breather, you could spend another twenty minutes jotting key messages under each section to 'smoke-test' and fine-tune the structure.
- The next time-burst could be focused on noting what data, diagrams and charts would support each section.
- You could spend the next few blocks writing content or drawing diagrams with proofreading and a final review in the last twenty minutes.

By using time boxes, you may also identify opportunities for others to help you. Perhaps you could outsource some of the content creation tasks to your colleagues. You can find plenty more on this subject in Chapter 2, 'Delivery: Delegation'.

Do What You Love to Stay Motivated

Regularly doing something you love is essential for generating the happiness chemicals you need whizzing around your brain to help you stay motivated. Some people call this work–life balance, but we don't like the word 'balance', as it implies equal proportions. We would much rather have disproportionate amounts of happiness, thank you very much.

That doesn't mean we should spend all day listening to music, but it might mean a few minutes listening to our favourite song at the end of a twenty-five-minute burst of work or going for a short walk in the sunshine to re-energize and clear our head. Working in bursts like this—often called the Pomodoro method after the classic kitchen timers that look like a Pomodoro tomato—can pay dividends in productivity.

Rest Is Crucial

You'll need to find your own optimal sleep level, but generally anything less than six hours, and you won't be firing on all cylinders. The best ideas often come after a good night's sleep. Your concentration will be far higher and your effectiveness in each of your time boxes will be multiplied, especially for creative tasks. As a bonus, you'll have much higher patience for the more mundane jobs.

So, ensure you factor adequate sleep into your usual routine to get the most out of your day. Although there will be days where emergencies take over, it shouldn't be the norm.

Just Do It

Procrastination—putting things off for another day—is one of the biggest time-destroyers. The more you put things off, the more daunting the tasks become, the more pressure you find yourself under to get them done as deadlines rapidly approach.

Earlier, we spoke about creating bursts of achievement. You can use the same principle to make a start on tasks. Once you have prioritized what you need to get done during a specific day, week or month, book a slot in your diary to make a start as soon as you can. Applying the principle of progress in short bursts and making small but tangible steps forward, you will lay a solid foundation to build on as you move forward.

Try this today with something you've been putting off. You may be surprised at how much satisfaction you get progressing on something you've been pushing to the back of your mind.

So, how do you make a start? Well, as the popular saying goes 'Just do it'. Start by writing down a brief plan of the approach you're going to take. Giving the task ahead of you some structure will provide you with a roadmap.

We have previously discussed the importance of a message that resonates in your heart and mind. If you want to be motivated to do something, have a dialogue with yourself about why it's important. Provide yourself with a couple of logical reasons for just doing it, but give your heart a little something too. Ask yourself, 'How great are you going to feel if you make a good start on this task today?'

If you can picture yourself feeling pleased or even relieved to have made a first skim through all those papers you were meaning to read, the desire for that positive feeling will help you make a start. It could be writing an essay, organizing a project, paying your bills, or even tidying your house. A warrior should never go into battle expecting defeat, but rather psych themselves up to believe they will conquer the enemy and emerge victorious.

Visualizing the win before the fight had begun was a favourite technique of Muhammad Ali, and it did him no harm—though the same cannot be said of his opponents!

Pick an important task you've been putting off and make a start on it today. Picture the feeling you'll get from achieving even a first pass and … just do it!

Blocking the Time-Destroyers

It's easy to say anything that isn't on your priority list is a waste of time, but in reality, we often have to spin several plates at once like undertaking routine tasks and maintaining relationships with our colleagues. It's less a matter of erasing time-destroyers and more a case of understanding which ones we need to manage and how to do so. In the simplest terms, there are three primary time-destroyers:

1. Pushy people: Those individuals who have zero awareness of other people's priorities and no issue interrupting you at the worst times.
2. Challenging chores: Tasks that are unrelated to the matter at hand but nevertheless can't be left to accumulate.

3. Digital distractions: All those e-mails and social media interactions that keep us connected at the cost of disconnecting us from our main purpose.

People

Most of us are social animals. We like to interact with colleagues and find our work relationships among the most enjoyable parts of our jobs. However, there is a difference between structured meetings and frequent, unpredictable interruptions. A good way to manage this is to combine the two by engaging in social interactions with a business purpose. Think of it as 'socializing with intent'.

At the beginning of a meeting or walking over to a colleague's desk, you can begin the interaction with some interesting talk such as 'How was the match the other day?' A brief chat on a fun topic you both like to talk about is incredibly beneficial for relationships and helps to depressurize the work environment. Then, simply follow on with a bit of business to make the whole interaction a productive use of both parties' time.

You may get a lot of random interruptions during the average day. If it's the nature of your business—for example, if you are a technical expert to whom a large number of people turn to for support throughout the day—you need to accommodate some degree of disruption. Leave space in your diary for people to come and talk to you or build flexibility into your schedule for those who need to take up a few minutes of your time.

Work out whichever method is most practical for you and stick to it. Having two or three slots in the day where you respond to your colleagues' requests may be worth a try, but it requires discipline. It's easier if you're setting time aside to respond to e-mails—say thirty minutes after lunch and thirty minutes before you go home. We will cover e-mail in much more detail later.

If batch-processing doesn't work for you for whatever reason, you should only be spending an hour or two responding to queries. Don't shy away from blocking out time to focus on work and advising colleagues that you'll come back to them shortly. Most people will understand if you are polite, and you keep your promise. Of course, if it genuinely is a two-minute question, you can use your discretion and respond immediately if you want to, especially if it's a team member whose work is held up waiting for an opinion from you.

Chores

We've all been there. Faced with a tough problem to solve, you see a less taxing task and decide to tackle that first. Sometimes, getting the easy stuff out of the way is a good idea, unless someone else could have done it for you and you're just using it as an excuse to avoid the tougher stuff—the jobs that require the skills the firm really values you for.

Maximizing your time in a core area where your organization needs you should be one of your key objectives most days. An example of this could be if you were a senior project manager and decided to focus on reorganizing your calendar instead of reviewing project plans or proposals. If you're lucky enough to have a personal assistant, you can be sure they'd do a better job of organizing your schedule.

You need to focus on delivering value for your organization. That is, after all, what you were hired for—not to say you can delegate all your administrative tasks, but all individuals, departments and organizations must find the appropriate balance between core tasks and routine jobs if they're to maximize their value.

Take a minute to look at your day today. Are you planning to spend a good amount of time on areas that exploit your core value to the firm? If not, try and minimize or delegate tasks that someone else could do. You'll find more on this in Chapter 2, 'Delivery: Delegation'.

Distractions

In our digitally connected world, surfing the net, checking social media or messaging friends is becoming addictive. The average person checks their phone over a hundred times a day. Even if it's only for thirty seconds, that is, fifty minutes a day checking your phone. Most of us acknowledge we spend at least that long if not longer tapping aimlessly at our screens.

Of course, there's great social value in connecting with friends, but if you spent hours of your day gossiping with colleagues, your boss would be quite rightly annoyed, so keep a lid on your social media and internet surfing time when at work. Try restricting it to lunch or tea breaks. Perhaps reward yourself after a burst of intensive, focused work with a quick peek at your phone. Leaving it out of reach when you don't plan to use it helps stiffen your resolve.

All three time wasters require a little discipline to kill off. Make a good start today by:

- Putting your smartphone away.
- Politely letting people know you're focused on a key task if they pop by.
- Spending more of your time delivering your core value.

Powering Up the Time-Creators

We have looked at the benefits to be gained by using every minute of your day effectively, but can you expand the day to make more time? Can you recruit more than your allotted 86,400 troops? Indeed, you can, and here are three ways of doing it:

1. Get more help
2. Use time zones

Get More Help

Delegating work and requesting help with large tasks can greatly expand the amount of time you have to manage other activities. Strong leaders maximize the number of tasks they can delegate by rationing their time to make it go further. It's particularly important for repetitive tasks. If your team is properly equipped, you'll create more time for yourself.

If you don't have a team that reports to you, consider sharing tasks with a colleague, assigning work to whoever can perform it most efficiently. For example, your colleague may be a number cruncher and you may be a PowerPoint guru, so why not do a deal where they help you with the numbers and you knock together some great-looking slides for them?

Priyesh recalls studying statistical economics at university, a weak subject for him but familiar ground for a friend who wasn't as strong as Priyesh in the essay-writing department. So, they chose to help each other, and both achieved a first in econometrics. If we can help each other out at school, why not at work or at home? All it takes is for us to be realistic and humble about where we need a little help and what we can offer in return.

In our connected world, you might even consider outsourcing work to a third party. On websites like freelancer.com, skilled remote workers can bid for tasks you need doing. Maybe you could pay someone to do your tax returns. That said, it doesn't always have to be tasks at work that need to be delegated. Sometimes, professional help at home like a cleaner or cook allows you to devote more time to spend with family or do more of the things you love.

Use Time Zones

Follow the Sun is a great technique for those working within a global team. As you start to wind down for the day, pass an ongoing task to a colleague in another location.

They can continue to work on it while you're asleep and hand it back to you as you wake the following day. Using this trick, you can effectively double your achievements.

Priyesh used this trick to deliver a near-impossible project. Using teams in New York, London and Singapore, he created what he called the 'thirty-six-hour day' by sharing tasks across the globe. Meanwhile, Alasdair managed teams in India, London and New York, designing work processes that allowed each team to begin their day with a workload passed on to them by colleagues a few thousand miles away.

Some trading houses manage global trading books, which get passed from one trader to another on the other side of the globe. They can manage the positions twenty-four hours a day, take full advantage of changing economic conditions, and benefit from arbitrage opportunities, that is, variances in market pricing between different locations.

However, a word of caution—using time zones will require you to make a concerted effort to communicate and keep enough overlap time to hand over work in enough detail so that it's seamless. Done incorrectly, this relay process can cause lengthy delays while one team waits to address unresolved issues left behind by the other.

Be More Effective

Spending five minutes looking for your keys, trying to remember something important you were meant to do, looking up a procedure you follow every day—all these things destroy time. Being more organized will save you time in the short term. Consider simple things like putting your essentials in the same place every time you get home. After all, a warrior who can't find their sword won't last long on the battlefield.

Keep a to-do list, ticking off items as you complete them and adding new ones as they arise. This basic tool can save you having to rack your brain trying to remember what it was you were supposed to do on a particular day. It doesn't matter if it's a paper diary or a digital app, just do it! An app will enable you to set priorities, deadlines and notifications, but keeping it simple is fine, as you'll probably have a reasonably good idea of what matters on a day-to-day basis.

Many organizations openly declare targets and goals. If you want to multiply the effectiveness and chances of meeting yours, tell the world what you're trying to achieve and by when. Making a public commitment will only add to your motivation.

Create a checklist for each project, as discussed in Chapter 3, 'Delivery: Managing Projects'. The more you plan tasks before executing them, the more likely you'll find a more efficient way to deliver the result. You can also confirm your approach with others, so you get the benefit of their perspective and perhaps their help with key tasks. Many organizations use checklists to help them execute repetitive tasks. Consider whether having a procedure in place can help take some of the memory work out of these duties for you and your team. It'll save time and ensure nothing is missed.

By being more organized, requesting help and using time zones, you'll find there is plenty more time available for you to get the most out of your day. Try applying some of these techniques with some of the key tasks on your plate right now.

E-mail Voodoo

There is a practical limit to the number of colleagues who can approach your desk over the course of a day, but there can be no end to the number of e-mails flooding your inbox, all clamouring for instant attention. E-mail is a tremendous form of communication that removes much of the need for time-chewing face-to-face meetings while establishing a paper trail of what's been said. But if you allow e-mails to dictate your time, you will be overwhelmed. There are many ways to manage what we call the e-maelstrom, but we have found these three particularly effective:

1. Prioritize your reaction
2. Keep a simple filing system
3. Process in bursts

Prioritize Your Reaction

An e-mail comes in. There's probably a temptation to respond immediately; after all, it's precisely what that fight or flight instinct discussed in Chapter 4, 'Controlling Your Emotions', programmes us to do. The arrival of an e-mail is a sudden event that demands our immediate attention. Unless we have a strategy for prioritizing our response, we may leave ourselves open to distraction, dropping whatever we're doing with every ping of our inbox. Beyond simply destroying time, we may find that our replies, hastily typed up in the heat of the moment, lack the nuance of a more measured response.

Priyesh remembers an invaluable piece of advice he received from one of his senior banking mentors, Peter Mellor, a senior derivatives trader in the City of London Investment Trust: 'When you've drafted a controversial or emotional e-mail that you are even slightly unsure of, hit save instead of send.' With this simple strategy, you can take a break and come back to the message after an hour or so. You'll have a chance to re-read the exchange and revise your initial reaction if you wish. Nine times out of ten, you'll make changes to the e-mail—or even delete it. You may decide to pick up the phone or talk to the person face-to-face, giving you the opportunity to adopt a softer, more human approach.

On the other hand, if your response is a straightforward answer to a question that doesn't require much thought, then go ahead and hit send, especially if holding off on a reply will negatively impact the other person's schedule. A good rule of thumb is that if you can respond to an e-mail in a couple of minutes, it's probably best to respond straight away.

But if a message is going to take longer because it needs a little more thought—or even actual data—for an informed response, try one of the following:

- Let the sender know you will get back to them and by when.
- Advise it might take a couple of days for you to gather the right information.
- Consider forwarding the e-mail to a colleague who can help.
- Flag the e-mail in your inbox so you don't forget about it.
- Give precedence to any queries hindering your team's progress.

Keep a Simple Filing System

The mantra for e-mail filing is to keep it simple. Try these four key categories:

1. Important: Any e-mails that require a more measured reply.
2. Actioned: Important mails you've already responded to.
3. Reference: Messages you want to refer back to in the future. Over time, you can create additional sub-folders like 'Industry News', 'Project Reference' and 'HR'.
4. Awaiting response: E-mail chains where you're waiting for a response.

This way, you can keep your primary inbox clutter-free and focus on new mail as it comes in. It may take time to get your mailbox sorted, but once you are on top of things, you will find it a time saver—even more so if you use e-mail for a sizeable chunk of your day-to-day work.

Burst-Processing

Earlier, we talked about dedicating twenty-minute bursts of effort to move a task forward and foster a continuous sense of achievement. Many senior leaders also reserve time-bursts to focus on responding to e-mails, mostly likely from their 'Important' file, so they can be given the appropriate level of attention. Some will do e-mails first thing in the morning before colleagues arrive and after they have set out their key priorities for the day. Some block out diary slots throughout the day or use their commuting time to and from work.

Whenever you choose to sort your e-mails, try to schedule a few dedicated time slots to tackle those trickier messages. Extend this to all mails that do not require urgent attention, and you'll finally be able to liberate yourself from being an e-mail responding machine!

This is what we call 'e-mail voodoo'. There is no single ideal approach. Instead, you must find the magic that works for you. It's well worth the time you'll spend figuring it out. A little discipline in how you deal with e-mails will make you far more productive.

To summarize:

- If you can respond immediately, do it.
- If you need more information, let the other person know you are going to respond—and when. Engage help as required, and flag the message.
- If your response is controversial, draft it, but wait a while before you hit send.

- Keep a simple filing system that reflects your priorities and supports your focus.
- Get into the habit of batch-processing your e-mails in bursts at set times each day.

Life-and-Death Prioritization

The final warrior-time–management principle is to have a myopic vision on the most important, mission-critical activities and allocate time accordingly. It's so easy to get bogged down with 'stuff', but time is our most valuable commodity. In a split second, a warrior must decide which moves will keep them alive and which will lead to defeat.

Identify the tasks that breathe life into your presence in the organization. Find those tasks which, if not performed well, may harm your career and, therefore, your ability to bring benefit to the organization—strategic initiatives that your organization values greatly and require the skills you have that set you apart from your colleagues.

These are the high-visibility tasks that you cannot afford to mess up, given their potential to damage your reputation, that of your department or, in some cases, the entire firm. They may not be the most interesting of challenges, but nevertheless, you should be highly motivated to meet them with all you have to offer. Other activities can be delayed. Peripheral battles can be fought another day. Multi-tasking is fine, but make sure you allow appropriate time to plan and execute these critical tasks first.

You may have noticed that this is a close cousin of the first warrior-time–management principle—knowing which battles need to be fought here and now and which ones can be relegated to the long-term war. This principle emphasizes the point that there are regular priorities, and there are life-and-death priorities. Ensure you know the difference and take bold steps to designate enough time to deal with the latter.

The Not-So-Subtle Steps

- Which battles are you going to fight today, and which can wait? Decide the top two or three things to focus on and keep them firmly in your mind. Allow yourself up to thirty minutes to think and plan.
- Organize your day so you can execute tasks in a time-boxed manner. Spend around twenty minutes on each task or part of a task. Aim to make tangible progress in each slot.
- Build in some time for fun activities during the day. Perhaps listen to a song you like to reward yourself after an intense burst of activity.
- Leave yourself enough time to rest—your brain will be far more productive.
- Don't put off hard tasks. Think of one or two logical reasons and an emotional reason as to why you need to just do it. Picture how good you will feel having completed a task. Plan how you'll start, key steps you'll take, and how you'll finish.
- Have a strategy to block out time-destroyers. Remember to socialize with intent, that is, use the preamble before a meeting to quickly catch up before getting down to business.
- If you're at high risk of interruptions in your job, either book a couple of slots in the day when you are most available for people and let them know or build a little flexibility into your calendar to allow for a reasonable number of questions. If you are focusing on a task, don't be shy to tell people you'll get back to them shortly so you can bank your achievement.
- Ensure that most of your time is focused on the core value you add to the firm and delegate other tasks that

can be handled by someone else. Keep control of digital distractions. Try to limit internet browsing, messaging and social media to break times, allowing you to keep your mind focused on the matter at hand.

- Use time-expansion techniques. Delegate or swap tasks with colleagues who are better at certain things than you. Consider drafting in extra resources from online freelancing websites. If you can, engage and coordinate teams across the world, ensuring strong handover communication with some overlap. Be more organized, whether that's putting your keys in the same place every day, pre-planning tasks, or having checklists that allow you to execute routine tasks faster.
- Use a little 'e-mail voodoo'. Your inbox should contain categories for e-mails you've 'Actioned', another for those 'Important' messages that will take a little more time, and one where you have sent a mail and are 'Awaiting Response'. Archive any e-mails you want to refer back to in the future in a separate 'Reference' folder.
- Avoid immediately hitting 'send' on a controversial or an emotionally charged e-mail. Draft a response, but come back to it later to review and amend it before sending.
- If a response is going to take less than a couple of minutes, get it out of the way, especially if it helps keep your team on track. If it's going to take longer, provide an estimated response time and place the message in your 'Important' file.
- Consider setting aside some time throughout your diary to burst-process mails, focus your efforts, and liberate yourself from your e-mails during the rest of your day.

- Make sure your 'life-and-death' priorities are taken care of first. Your reputation and that of your firm are key assets. Tasks of high importance and visibility should be given priority. Dedicate your time to activities that breathe life into the organization.

As the name implies, 'warrior time management' requires a ruthless approach in order to make the best possible use of our most valuable commodity—time. It is worth the effort, so make a great start today and begin conquering time.

PART TWO

BUILDING TRUST

6

Managing Client Relationships

- *What's the most effective way to sell to a client?*
- *What's the best way to develop a relationship that delivers future business?*
- *How do you close a sale or strike a deal every time?*

We are often told to be 'client-centric', but what does that really mean? Selling to a client means a lot more than simply offering a proposal and signing a deal, although that's obviously a favourable result. Building an effective client relationship is vital if you want to continually provide positive business outcomes for all concerned. Ask yourself:

- Who is your client?
- Who do you sell to?
- Who should you sell to?

- Why should you sell to them now?
- Why should they buy from you now?
- What is in it for them?
- What is in it for you?
- What differentiates you from your competitors?

Being able to answer these kinds of questions is a crucial component of any mutually beneficial sales relationship, which is the best kind of sales relationship!

In our experience, great salespeople sell to both people *and* the organizations they belong to. Their client is a person; someone they connect with whose interests, challenges and motivations they understand. However, the organization is also their client, and they will aim to support its macro objectives and commercial interests. Relating to your client on both a personal and organizational level creates a solid foundation for future business.

You also need to know which clients *not* to engage with. There are certain types of clients we're happy to serve and others we may prefer not to do business with. Ultimately, a client is a sales tool. Potential clients will look at who you already sell to when considering whether to buy from you; they will recoil if they see you do business with a company with questionable ethics or commercial practices.

This chapter is mainly about winning commercial business for your firm from other organizations within the marketplace. However, most of the principles we're going to discuss also apply to relationships within your own company. Every worker in every organization is selling their skills to an internal client. It could be their direct boss or the head of a department that benefits from their work.

When it comes to promoting your own career interests and progressing towards professional goals, the art of selling is key. We'll look at this aspect of career management in more detail in Chapter 10, 'The Business of You'

Build a Network Map of Your Clients

Information is vital for improving your odds of winning a new client. Information helps you to hone your pitch so it has the best chance of success—from deciding whom to approach to how you address them and all the way down to the decision-makers deeper in the client organization. Once you've identified which companies may be interested in your product or service, your next step is getting to the right person.

It's a journey, and although it may start with a cold call to say something like, 'Hi, I'm calling from PWV Consulting. We're offering a new credit card risk management solution that we thought may be of interest to you ...' it's very unlikely to end there.

Brute-force tactics won't get you anything other than a click and a dial tone. Effective salespeople work by building a network of contacts across the industry and asking for help to get to the right person. We will discuss more about building an effective network in Chapter 7, 'Building a Network'. Think of your network as a map of your contacts and sales prospects. It is more than a list of names; it represents the needs and interests of those people, the details of the business they are in, and the relationships that exist between them. Ask yourself these questions:

- Who are their competitors?
- Where do they sit in the organizational structure?
- Who can they introduce you to?
- What decisions are they responsible for?
- Who might help you make a sale?

It is also a record of your interactions with prospects and the next steps you're planning to take. When building your own network map, you need to ensure that you balance nurturing relationships with your current contacts by scanning the horizon for future opportunities.

In fact, every person you meet in this networked world is a potential client—or someone who can connect you with one. Resources such as LinkedIn, the social network for professionals, can provide leads, but there is no substitute for understanding a client through interactions with their peers or colleagues. Use any time you have with clients to enrich your network map, utilizing whatever knowledge they are willing to share.

Every sale starts with a pitch. Securing the opportunity to make your pitch is the first hurdle you need to overcome. As a senior client himself—and one with an incredibly busy schedule—Priyesh acknowledges that he's incredibly difficult to pin down for a meeting. He recognizes that persistence pays off but, at the same time, he appreciates that the more tailored the approach, the better the chance of a productive connection.

Turn Up the Heat on Cold Mails

Sending an unsolicited e-mail only tends to work if, by a stroke of luck, you happen to nail a burning problem the recipient is facing at that precise moment. Like cold calling, it's a poor way to get a client's attention. However, if you find yourself limited to this route, your cold mail should be as personalized as possible to understand who the contact is and what may interest them. From the prospective client's point of view, seeing a reference from someone they know and respect helps to create trust.

A personalized cold e-mail may look something like this:

Dear Mr Jones,

Apologies for the unsolicited e-mail. We've not met before, but I understand you manage the Finance Department at ABM Bank.

I recently met with Mr Martin, head of finance at SBR Bank. He expressed a great deal of interest in using our services to enhance SBR's accrual accounting approach to meet the new MIFID rules. I thought I'd reach out in case this is of interest to you as well.

Could I perhaps have thirty minutes in your diary to understand your perspective on this and share some ideas with you? If you have no objections, I can make the arrangements with Lucy, or I'll try to call you in the next couple of days.

Best regards.

There are two key points to note here.

We've written the mail in a straightforward, down-to-earth manner, highlighting that there are good reasons for the connection. Despite the e-mail being unsolicited, which we've apologized for, it has been personalized to a great extent. Through the e-mail we have attempted to understand the contact's role, which is where sources like LinkedIn and our network map database become essential.

The stronger the reference, the more likely it is that the contact will pay attention to the e-mail and note its relevance to them. You would need Mr Martin's consent to use his name, of course. The reference becomes even more powerful if you can get permission from Mr Martin to say something along the lines of 'he recommended I reach out to you'.

It's subtle, but you've also sown the seed that you have a positive professional connection with 'Lucy', your prospective client's personal assistant. Without these direct, individual references, your message will read like a typical cold mail and probably end up in the garbage. If you can't secure a specific reference, you can always include the name of competitor firms, modifying your message to something like:

> I've recently met with three other banks, including SBR, ABM and NatEast, and they've shown a great deal of interest in using our services to help enhance their accrual accounting approach to meet the new MIFID rules. I thought I would take the liberty of reaching out in case this is of interest to you as well.

To relate the message even more closely to the client, you could recognize and appreciate a recent achievement or contribution. Perhaps they wrote an article, or you heard them speak at a conference somewhere. Although people quickly see through empty flattery, a little genuine appreciation can go a long way.

If we have understood our potential client—where they sit in the industry and who their peers, competitors and connections are—then we have a better chance of connecting with them. Even with the most careful honing, your cold mail's chance of success is probably only around 10–20 per cent, but that's much better odds than a generic, copy-paste e-mail devoid of personal context or any indication that you understand the client.

Engage by Event

Another great way of connecting with clients is by attending industry events. You can try to simply 'bump into' a new prospect at a conference, but a powerful way to make it a bit more certain is to either invite them to an event that you have organized or to someone else's as your guest. It would be even more engaging to invite the client to participate as a speaker or panellist, assuming they have some genuine industry expertise.

This provides multiple benefits:

- The client gets an opportunity to network.
- The industry gets the benefit of their perspective.
- You get quality time to engage with them.

This approach requires some investment, but it's a great relationship-builder. If done right, the person organizing the event is not only delivering value to multiple clients but also building a reputation in the market as someone in the know—or trying to be, at least.

While the event should be about building a bond, once it's all over, it's worthwhile trying to share some ideas with the client and perhaps organize a follow-up meeting. We all understand the nature of business, so asking for an opportunity to understand a client's needs more or share your thoughts on potential avenues of collaboration is perfectly reasonable once you have established a relationship.

Whichever way you do it, establishing a broad network across your industry is essential for making sales. One senior partner at a top-four consultancy firm has a small portfolio of particularly high-value clients but still maintains a large network to stay connected and build on his knowledge of the industry. If he limited his circle to just those high-value clients, generating new business would be far more difficult. By broadening his contacts, he increases his probability of knowing when a prospect needs his services.

Have Jumbo Ears

Understanding where someone sits in their organization and what challenges they face is essential. It means you can put your offering into context so they can clearly see its value to them and their organization. After all, they will need to be able to sell your solution or service to their colleagues and seniors before they can sign on the dotted line.

To do this, you need first to be prepared to listen *actively*—that is, listen, ask questions about what you've heard, and then listen some more.

There are two ways we can be persuaded to close a deal, whether it's for a new umbrella or a multi-million-dollar computer system. The first is emotional impulse—we like the salesperson, or we're attracted to the product on the spur of the moment. As a sales strategy, chasing such impulses is unreliable and often futile.

Alternatively, we may have a compelling need that the product or service promises to satisfy. Think about it, shops sell way more umbrellas when it is raining.

Active listening allows you to discover the client's current needs and highlight the features of your product best suited to address those needs. Once you understand what the client is looking for, you may be able to adapt an existing service to serve their requirements better than your current offering. You may uncover an opportunity to explain how your product goes beyond the clients' immediate needs to provide benefits they did not anticipate.

However, be careful not to make assumptions. You will never know your client better than they know themselves. Instead, you might say something like, 'We've seen many clients benefit significantly from doing this. Does it sound like it might be of interest to you?'

Active listening might also highlight that your product is *not* suited to the client's current challenge. If so, you can turn this to your advantage by acknowledging the fact and respecting their time. Leave them with some understanding of your offering and express an interest in catching up again in a few months' time.

Active listening provides targeted questioning to help tailor a solution, which is an extremely effective tool. Say you go to a car showroom to buy a small car. A great salesperson will want to sell you the biggest car they can and stretch you to the limits of your budget. To do this, they'll probably ask you something like, 'Why is it that you want to buy a small car?'

You insist that you only need a runabout for getting into town and back. They ask how many there are in your family, and you reply it's for you and your two children. The salesperson shows you a little car that meets your needs but adds that, for your family's comfort, you may want to consider a larger model.

While selling the features of the bigger car in terms of how it would benefit you and your family, they share what their own kids love about it. Then they invite your kids to jump in and ask if you want to go for a test drive. They'll ask your kids what they think, and obviously, they'll love it! You've inadvertently become totally invested in this car.

You may be apprehensive, as the cost is higher than anticipated. A great salesperson will recognize this and want to understand your budget better. They will offer you financing terms that could bring the cost within the limits of your budget. In fact, a clever salesperson would probably persuade you that financing a bigger car gives you more value for money, spreads your cost and provides you with more benefits overall.

You may ask the salesperson for a discount and, to close the deal, they might make a time-limited offer. It sounds cheesy but a salesperson willing to go out of their way to meet your needs can encourage you to close the deal. It appeals to the buyer's heart, and their ego too. If the salesperson can't improve the terms, they'll take great pains to explain how they would love to give you a better deal but are constrained by factors beyond their control.

This may not be the typical transaction you face at work, but it demonstrates the key principles of using your jumbo ears to sell:

- Actively listen to your client's needs and understand their situation.
- Advise based on what your client tells you, not just on what you want to sell.
- Adapt and tailor your product to the client.
- If your offering isn't a good fit at the time, be transparent about it.
- Consider extending the offer to propose more benefits for the client.
- Maybe get other people in the client's team to buy into the features.
- Show flexibility and a desire to help the client.
- Assure them that you've stretched the offer as far as possible.
- If possible, close the deal with a sweetener to build goodwill.
- Provide excellent after-sales support to pave the way for a future sale.

Let the Client Know You

Though it is critical that you show a good understanding of your client and their organization, the client will be equally impressed by your awareness of your own firm. A good service provider understands everything about their own organization and is happy to discuss both its strengths and areas where its offerings may require further development. Like a good salesperson, a good service provider knows their market, and their organization's place within it.

Many clients like to be reassured that a salesperson knows their business and not just how to sell. You can build confidence by sharing some relevant experience and related industry knowledge. It is essential that, as a service provider, you can communicate:

- The value you aim to provide
- Your core offering

- How you differentiate yourself from competitors
- The relationship you want with the client's organization

You should aim to have a strong elevator pitch, as described in Chapter 1, 'Communicating 360'. It is important that your identity is clear, so the client feels they are dealing with a company that knows its niche. Attractive presentation materials that support and detail your organization's credentials and capabilities are indicative of the quality clients can expect from you, so it's well worth investing in the right 'look and feel' to reflect your standards.

Be an Adviser First

The first step to building a relationship with a client is breaking the ice. Everyone has extracurricular interests outside work. Wise salespeople ask about these activities and maybe even share some relevant insights of their own. Connecting with clients and prospects on a human level is crucial. Business is done with people first and organizations second. Whatever it may be, connecting on a non-business-related topic is worth the effort.

Another key attribute of a great sales executive is the ability to share business knowledge and perspectives with their clients, providing value beyond any potential contract discussion that's on the table. A good salesperson should know the following:

- Major trends in the industry
- What the client's competitors are doing
- Innovations the client may not know about

The highest aim of a salesperson is to demonstrate they are a trusted adviser—someone the client can turn to for friendly support and wise insight, as well as valuable goods or services. Many bankers, consultants and other service providers devote a great deal of time to building such relationships with their key clients. When the time is right, these connections provide an opportunity to do business that benefits both sides.

There are three reasons why the trusted adviser role is so powerful:

1. You've spent so much time with your client, so you will be in the strongest possible position to understand and respond to any challenges they face.
2. There is a good chance they will call you first when they need advice or a sounding board. They may even float an idea that could lead to a sale.
3. You can gather valuable market insights, use any non-confidential elements to build your network map and then share it with other clients. This is a virtuous circle.

This is relevant across your client's organization. It is important to build strong relationships with the key decision-makers and high-ranking members of their teams. It's no secret that the best leaders consult their teams when selecting a solution provider.

Every Little Helps

Never miss an opportunity to support a client. Sometimes, even a seemingly trivial amount of assistance can be priceless when it comes to building trust and enhancing your client relationship. Everybody has limited time. If a client has turned to you or you know there is something you can do make their lives easier, helping them should be your top priority, though you must never compromise your or your organization's reputation to do so.

This philosophy also applies to small things like participating in client team events, sending your client articles and research that may be of interest to them, and remembering occasions like birthdays. If your company policy allows for it, corporate hospitality can also provide a platform outside the work environment for building better client relationships. A quick catch-up over a coffee now and again to find out what's going on in their world and share a little about yours can significantly deepen a bond with a client.

The Not-So-Subtle Steps

Be the best partner you can be using the following tools to sharpen your approach:

- Know your client by taking time to fully research and understand your network map. Build a knowledge database that includes information about your client's industry, what matters to them and where you can add value.
- Add heat to a cold call or mail by personalizing it with a relevant industry reference, as well as thoughts specific to the individual's position and a follow-up request.
- Engage clients through events like industry functions. Organizing such an event can create fantastic opportunities to connect with multiple clients and provide a less pressurized environment for exchanging ideas.
- Maintain a wide network of clients to avoid having all your eggs in one basket.
- Actively listen to your clients' needs and tailor solutions to meet them. Using targeted questioning helps the client see the benefit of your offering. Close the sale by providing the right solution and include a sweetener where possible.
- Always show intent to do your best for the client's organization and your own. Follow up after the sale to ensure satisfaction and continue to build the relationship.

- Ensure the client knows what you stand for and your value proposition.
- Build trust by being transparent about your limitations.
- Be an adviser first. Provide industry knowledge, research and insights. Spend time with the client, sharing thoughts and offering help.
- Understand your client so you can tailor your offering to their unique needs.
- Help whenever you can, especially when a client asks. Seek opportunities to support them and build a partnership without an expectation of immediate business.

You can apply most of these principles to internal dealings as well. The big difference is, there's no need to be as formal or shy of unsolicited contact when it comes to colleagues. Most employers encourage a collaboration culture, and the rules of the road are largely the same—know your client, adapt your solution to their needs, be a trusted adviser, ensure they know your strengths, help them wherever possible and sell them the right solution.

All the best strengthening your client relationships and closing those sales!

7

Building a Network

- *Have you ever been told that you need to be more visible?*
- *Do you feel like your organization doesn't fully recognize or support you?*
- *Is your boss avoiding your promotion because of your low profile?*
- *Do you have limited channels to seek advice or new opportunities?*

Building a broad network across your organization and industry opens countless doors that lead to support, opportunities and potential sales. An effective network goes far beyond having thousands of connections on social media—although a decent, up-to-date profile on LinkedIn is essential and a fantastic place to start.

The best leaders form and nurture connections by building mutually beneficial relationships and connecting regularly on professional, social and virtual levels. This can be rewarding and pleasurable and also accrue professional benefits. After all, we do spend a large chunk of our lives at work, no matter how carefully we cultivate our work–life balance.

Building and maintaining strong professional relationships takes a great deal of time and attention. Like the tasks your employer assigns to you, this is work, and you will reap rewards proportionate to the effort you put in.

You may be fortunate enough to work for a company that understands the importance of networking and provides a nurturing environment in which to do so. There are many ways a company can foster an atmosphere of cross-collaboration; for example, by team-building exercises, 'brown bag' lunches and sponsoring company sports teams.

Employees often find their own ways of networking as well. Alasdair fondly remembers the local pubs where he and his colleagues would head for regular after-work drinks—within walking distance of the office but still discreetly out of view.

When building your network, there are three terrains you need to focus on. First, and probably the most overlooked, having a solid network within your own team allows your network to be flexible and responsive to challenges as they arise. Second, building strong connections across the firm helps you build your profile and gain support for initiatives.

Finally, having a broad matrix of contacts across your industry and into adjacent sectors is essential for building your knowledge base. Think of it as the intelligence network that keeps you informed and allows you to act beyond the immediate reach of your role.

In each of these terrains, there are key tools leaders use to build good connections. Just as a transport network utilizes roads, railways, signals and traffic lights to move goods and people from place to place, our network needs certain components to function properly.

First, we need to connect all the roads and rails, which requires both a one-time effort like an introduction or kick-off meeting, as well as continuous maintenance of the connections via regular catch-ups. We also need to ensure the traffic flows smoothly between each of the network points, such as by sharing information, providing help and requesting insights.

We can use signals to route traffic across the network; for example, building ad-hoc groups like task forces, think-tanks and expert panels. The value of a network is that it greatly increases the resources you can call on to address any given challenge.

First Terrain: Networking Begins at Home

To start with, let's look at some examples of how the most effective practitioners use these tools to build and leverage networks within their own teams. Whether you're the manager or a team member, your foremost responsibility is to work well within the team. To achieve this, effective leaders and team players must engage in three things.

1. Have regular one-on-one meetings with other team members. This can be weekly, bi-weekly or monthly. It may seem like overkill when the team is already interacting most days, if not every day. However, taking the time to step outside the project you're currently engaged in is an opportunity to deepen relationships or defuse any tensions.
2. 'Put money in the bank' with colleagues by helping them out, sharing insights and seeking guidance. Priyesh recalls one senior manager who openly shared his opinions to dismantle boundaries between himself and others, creating a feeling that he is straightforward and down-to-earth. This type of interaction builds a strong bond of trust and others repay this openness with their own honesty, something that is incredibly valuable in any corporate environment.
3. Play a facilitation role by organizing meetings to discuss a topic or work on an initiative not directly related to the task at hand. Alternatively, you could be the social organizer who brings the

team together for a good cause—to celebrate success or just connect as a group.

These techniques help to create a healthy team spirit and facilitate further connections. Creating this kind of network also helps to solidify the organizer's position as a leader and a good person to work with—as someone who builds a positive fabric in the team.

Second Terrain: Network Your Organization

These points apply equally as much when networking across your organization. The key difference is choosing whom to connect with and when to do so. The higher you climb up the corporate ladder, the more time you should be spending networking, whether with your broader department, your boss's peers or the organization as a whole.

Monthly or even quarterly catch-ups are perfectly sufficient for staying connected with peers who may be performing a similar role to you or colleagues on shared projects.

Think of this as a stakeholder matrix that contains all the people you're either working with or would like to connect with. It may be no more than an informal sketch, but you should consider documenting all the key information. You could include details like your sense of what the stakeholder thinks of you, what they might want from you and what you can give them. Consider how frequently you should refresh contact and consider the best way to connect with them given the nature of your relationship.

Remember, their time is as precious as yours, so you will have to choose your moments wisely. Perhaps make a mental note to engage them briefly after a meeting or invite them to a social event. When it comes to requesting more formal or regular catch-ups, the most effective networkers aren't afraid to ask. However, it's good etiquette to request a catch-up only if you feel it would be of mutual benefit. Where the person is senior to you, a request for their mentorship may be a good way to connect.

Like most things in life, an awareness of who you should stay connected with and how often will drive you to take the initiative. However, you'll probably need thick skin. If people don't always respond positively, it may be that they don't have the time or the need at that moment. Either way, the fact that you want to build a bridge will rarely work against you.

Third Terrain: Extend Your Reach

Finally, you should reach out beyond the boundaries of your organization. Although all the principles we've discussed so far continue to apply, time constraints mean it's important to be resourceful when dedicating time to this terrain.

Effective leaders connect directly with people working for other organizations in their field, be they consultants, industry peers or ex-colleagues. Even meeting some of these people a few times a year can be enough to keep you up to date with important trends—those early-warning signs that allow you to position yourself for what's coming. It also keeps you in the sights of those who may one day be able to provide advice, assistance or employment.

When Alasdair moved from full-time employment to freelance engagements, the industry-spanning network he'd built was key to keeping a steady flow of work coming in. A powerful way to initiate this is to organize an industry-level forum or catch-up. It's an investment, but it can pay dividends for building closer relationships (see the section on engaging through events in Chapter 6, 'Managing Client Relationships').

Consultancies often use this technique to bring leaders together around a subject of mutual interest. Events like these keep relationships fresh and the organizer at the front of the mind.

Attending conferences, industry forums or training courses is a great way to pick up a few connections who you can follow up with on a selective basis. Don't be shy about inviting them to connect with you on social media. It's important to reiterate that you are on display at these events. You will make an impression, so make sure it's a positive one.

When meeting socially, don't miss an opportunity to develop a contact with mutual interests and follow up professionally afterwards. Another key element of building bonds is meeting on a social level; for instance, organizing drinks or dinner with like-minded people to deepen your bond with them.

There's always a professional aspect to these interactions, but sometimes, simply having fun cements a relationship and makes doing business a little more pleasurable for all. Use this technique sparingly though. There's a fine line between the odd social occasion with a bit of 'shop talk' and doing it so often you're branded a total bore, never to be invited out again!

Get Value from Your Network

Regardless of the terrain you're looking to build a network on, you should form a clear view of what you want from the interaction before you engage. Like most things in life—especially in business—a little preparation goes a long way.

Decide what key messages and facts about your team, initiatives and progress you would like to share. To put our own twist on a social media term, think of it as going 'selectively' viral. Spread positive information about your achievements, challenges and initiatives across your team, organization and wherever else it's relevant in the industry. According to an interesting theory, if you deliver a piece of information to three people in three different channels, you will eventually hear it back from an entirely different source.

Identify the information that would be of particular importance to your contact, based on your initiatives, the changes in your own organization and industry trends they may not be aware of. Don't forget, the information you have may be useful to your contacts, but you still owe a debt of discretion to your colleagues, clients and employer. Spilling trade secrets is unlikely to win you many friends and may even land you in hot water.

It's human nature to gossip but do so with caution. It demonstrates openness, but it can also win you a reputation as someone who can't be trusted, which would be fatal for your career. Warren Buffett once said, 'Never do anything in life if you would be ashamed of seeing it printed on the front page of your hometown newspaper for your friends and family to see.'[2] Wise words, indeed.

Without making it seem too premeditated or becoming the one-trick pony who always tells the same stories, it's beneficial to maintain a constantly updated store of facts, tales and humour that makes the experience richer and more fun for those who interact with you.

Ask your connections for advice, opinions or help. Networking is a fantastic opportunity to gather information and most people are quite happy to provide a perspective. Listen carefully—the insight of a trusted contact is a precious resource.

Finally, don't forget to ask to arrange for further meetings if there are things you would like to explore in more detail or requests you would like to flesh out. See Chapter 2, 'Delivery: Delegation', for more on this topic. This way, you create fertile ground on which to

---

2   Peter Gasca, Inc, 'Warren Buffett's Super Simple Advice For Becoming Successful', *Insider*, https://www.businessinsider.com/warren-buffett-advice-for-success-2014-8?IR=T

cultivate relationships and establish a worthwhile reason for your next meeting.

The Not-So-Subtle Steps

To further expand your network:

- List the key individuals in your ecosystem: your team, organization, industry and social circle. Identify what they think of you, what you'd *like* them to think of you, what you can offer them, how they can help you and how to connect with them.
- Pull together key messages about yourself, your team and your organization. Interesting stories and funny anecdotes are perfect for sharing. But remember, a lack of spontaneity will work against you, so don't flesh your patter out too much.
- Identify three key people in your team, three in your wider organization and three industry figures you want to create a relationship with. Having established a connection, make a note to reconnect on a regular basis.
- Look for opportunities to organize a gathering of like-minded individuals at least twice a year, where you can be the anchor and facilitate the discussion. You can also be more relaxed and organize a social networking event to connect people.
- When you're ready for your next move, leverage your network to ask for advice or opinions. It could be through these interactions that you find your next opportunity.

We hope you have fun reaching out to people and enriching your network.

8

Managing Up

- *Do you sometimes feel your boss doesn't 'get' you?*
- *Are you concerned they won't promote you because of it?*
- *Do you think your manager supports your peers more than they support you?*
- *Do you sometimes find yourself arguing with your boss?*

Your boss is one of the biggest catalysts of your career. Understanding what matters to them and those above them in the hierarchy is a critical factor for your success. In a modern company, authority flows in two directions. A company is nothing more than a collection of people whose contrasting areas of expertise come together in pursuit of a common mission.

It could be offering consumers a portfolio of goods and services, generating a profit for shareholders or fulfilling some other community aim on behalf of the organization's employees or customers. The key point is that it cannot be achieved without all the specialities represented throughout the workforce. Marketing creates the demand, operations creates the product, finance handles the cash, sales brings in clients and so on.

Across a company, each employee is hired to add their skills into the mix, and their unique knowledge gives them the authority to represent their field of expertise. This is known as horizontal authority. It runs across the organization without recognizing anyone's length of service, salary or the view from their office window. When the CEO arrives in the morning, it may be up to a junior security guard to let them in.

The other type of authority is the more traditional, top-down kind. For the firm's collection of skills to be deployed efficiently, there is a hierarchy of roles. For example, the marketing director coordinates and leads the marketing team, while the senior management team sets out a strategy for the company as a whole, under the direction of the CEO.

We've discussed navigating the horizontal landscape at great length already, working with colleagues within your function and beyond— even beyond the borders of the organization. This chapter is about the top-down hierarchy and, in particular, how to work effectively with the person immediately above you—your boss. There is no relationship more important in your professional life. Get it right, and this relationship will accelerate your progress. Get it wrong, and you could find your career coming to a complete standstill.

Key to managing this relationship is recognizing that organizations work to achieve targets. A company's senior staff has a greater command of these overarching goals and are motivated to demonstrate tangible progress. In simple terms, your job is to help your boss meet these targets to make them look good in front of their boss. Doing it successfully will make you an asset, both to your boss and the organization as a whole.

Agree on Priorities: What, How and When?

To effectively manage your relationship with your boss, address these three questions about how you're going to work together:

1. *What* are you trying to achieve?
2. *How* will you go about achieving it?
3. *When* will your efforts pay off?

If you're ever unclear on any of these questions, ask your boss to explain what they currently see as your key priorities and how these priorities lead into the organization's broader mission. Ask your boss how they see you best contributing to these goals.

Better still, use your own initiative to propose ways you and your team can provide support. Being proactive and brainstorming ideas that underpin and enhance your department's contribution to the organization's targets is incredibly powerful. You are, in effect, helping your boss with their own leadership task.

Once you have agreed on your targets, set clear benchmarks so both of you are completely aligned on what success looks like. For example:

- Will you deliver a project by a certain date? If so, set the deadline.
- What will your specific, quantifiable contribution be?
- Are there any key deliverables that will help the organization?

For example, you might be an analyst who normally provides data, but you may also commit to providing additional recommendations from your analysis, adapting and developing your contribution beyond what it was previously.

Confirm that your boss agrees with your goals, and then plan how you will jointly measure progress. Begin your collaborative journey by singing from the same hymn sheet.

Share a Game Plan

Once you've agreed *what* you're aiming to achieve, set out clear targets and deadlines. You should agree on *how* you plan to deliver the goods.

- What steps will you take?
- Who else will you involve?
- What support will you need?

With the *what* and the *how* clear in your mind, set expectations on *when* your boss will see tangible results and how frequently you'll be keeping them updated. Will you provide a weekly status report or opt for a monthly deep dive? It doesn't have to be too rigid. Don't be afraid to go off the beaten track, cancelling meetings altogether where there's nothing substantial to report or arranging an extra catch-up if things change. Just be specific about the schedule to keep the programme on track and your work noticed.

You can help your boss market these plans by creating materials that highlight your initiative to those higher up in the organization. As you achieve your goals, you should be presenting updates that demonstrate tangible progress, both quantitatively and qualitatively. In particular, highlight where you and your team are overachieving. Your performance against your targets acts as a running commentary of your suitability for promotion. Make sure those responsible for influencing your future path are aware of your potential.

Given the tendency for the best-laid plans to go awry, be ready to take your boss's advice or suggest mitigating strategies of your own if you're falling behind or veering off course. The last thing any boss wants is a nasty surprise and bad news to deliver to their own superiors. A transparent, consistent and collaborative approach will build a bridge of trust between you and your boss as you work together towards your shared goals.

Building Rapport

Aim to develop a professional relationship with your boss. Aligning goals and sharing progress will provide a strong foundation, but there is more you can do. If you're fully supporting your boss, you will be willing and able to step in when other professional challenges arise, or a trustworthy opinion is needed. Showing this kind of support transforms a relationship between superior and subordinate into more of a partnership, which will be more satisfying and productive for both of you. However, in seeking this partnership, be careful not to overstep the bounds of hierarchy. Use the time you have together to learn as much as possible about what they do and how they do it. However, trying too hard to establish yourself at their level will deny you this opportunity and probably damage their trust in you to boot.

The key here is finding a balance between helping to develop and implement your boss's ideas and doing some of the thinking for them. Like any relationship, these partnerships are most effective when they bring out the best in both parties. You should either fully support their decision or offer an alternative perspective—'offer' being the operative word, not impose.

Being in a position of seniority, your boss may have a wider perspective that you're not aware of—and they may not be able to share. Even if they don't take your advice, you should be seen actively supporting their cause, whatever it may be.

Developing a Relationship

Building rapport creates more varied interactions than a purely professional relationship, which can be rewarding given the amount of time we spend at work. Where possible, don't be shy to seek shared ground, whether that be over hobbies, interests or family situations. Maybe you both enjoy the same sport, have kids of similar ages, or share a passion for art?

Embrace opportunities to spend time connecting outside of work. Connecting at a human level helps to build a foundation of understanding that will repay the time and effort you expend tenfold. It will also make work a more enjoyable experience for both of you and reduce the need for those awkward exchanges of small talk about the weather or the bins.

Of course, professional boundaries still apply. Be careful not to sully any professional goodwill by being indiscreet. For example, you may be a passionate supporter of Manchester United Football Club—heaven help you!—while your boss has been a fan of arch-rival Liverpool since childhood. While some tongue-in-cheek banter and competition are fun and healthy, you cannot risk allowing emotions to spill over into your work life.

Humankind has evolved to hunt in packs over the course of millennia. Your aim is to build and maintain that group bond but to be able to express your unique identity when it really counts. Remember, though it's great to form a personal relationship with your boss, you should respect the position they hold in the organizational hierarchy. That responsibility is their own until they choose to delegate any part of it to you or anyone else.

Promote Yourself

As you focus on hitting targets and building rapport with your boss, don't forget, your boss is rarely the only decision-maker when it comes to giving you more responsibility. Often, promotions and pay increases are influenced by your boss's peers and superiors—and sometimes, even by clients with whom you have dealings.

That's why the three methods we discussed so far—sharing a game plan, building rapport and developing a relationship—apply not only to your immediate boss but also to other senior staff members who could influence your progression.

There is more on how to build a bond with these colleagues in Chapter 7, 'Building a Network'. Within the context of managing up, it is essential you know who the decision-makers are in your organization so you can build the appropriate profile with them, recruiting your boss to your cause wherever appropriate.

If your boss has several peers at the same level as them, you should consider what they are likely to say about you and, indeed, what *their* boss might say about you. You should explicitly build this goal into your personal game plan. Lean on your boss to help get you invited to key meetings, where projects you are working on are being discussed, for example. While you may not be able to get on everyone's radar, you need some allies in this group who can support you in these meetings, aside from your immediate superior.

This is not an easy process and requires deliberate effort on your part. However, there are some techniques that can help. If you've had a particularly successful engagement with a client, don't hesitate to ask them for feedback, calling out your performance and that of your department. Proactive leaders don't shy away from feedback, whether it's 'putting in a good word' or seeking confirmation that there's nothing else you can help with.

You can also build rapport while you're involved in your firm's broader initiatives, such as a cross-departmental project for which one of your manager's peers is an ambassador. Build a bond by talking about your team's progress and offer to share ideas or tools with their team. Don't be embarrassed about using such events for brazen self-promotion. It's one of the reasons why organizations are so keen to hold them in the first place! Everyone wins when members of an organization have opportunities to broaden their relationships and their understanding of each other's roles and personalities.

However you achieve this, it's your job to build your profile and 'put money in the bank' with people across the organization— people who are then far more likely to support your boss when they put you up for promotion.

Where you've had positive interactions with peers or your supervisor's peers, let your boss know so they can also build their confidence in you and help to further reinforce those positive perceptions. If there are times when things haven't quite worked out as expected, it's just as important to make your boss aware. They can help remedy the situation or put things in perspective when the time comes to talk about your performance.

Contingency Planning

As with all situations where there is a risk of things going off the boil, agreeing on a contingency plan with your boss to mitigate any risk is essential. In such situations, experience counts. Brainstorming what could go wrong with someone more senior will help you construct a plan to manage potential problems if these risks materialize.

Priyesh has never forgotten an extremely valuable piece of advice he was given by his father, a senior banker. He would always tell his team, 'If you have a problem and you keep it to yourself, it's yours to solve. If you share it with me, then it's mine.' It's a simple, common-sense principle along the lines of 'a problem shared is a problem halved'.

When you share a possible challenge with an experienced boss in a constructive manner, you benefit from their experience and mitigate your own risk too. Of course, coming to the table with potential solutions keeps you in the frame as a proactive leader.

The Not-So-Subtle Steps

Here's how to forge a winning partnership with your boss:

- Agree on common goals with your boss—*what* you need to achieve, by *when* and *how*.
- Update your boss on your progress regularly and create presentation materials to promote your achievements across the organization.
- Be a supportive partner to your boss. Help them develop and execute ideas and provide them with thoughts and insights to build a professional collaboration.
- Connect with your boss on all levels. Share common professional goals, interests and social time to develop a healthy yet appropriate personal relationship.
- Promote yourself by building relationships with those who can influence your progression and nurture trust. Let your boss know so they too can champion your cause.
- Manage risks transparently and jointly. Seek advice from senior colleagues and opt for a proactive approach, taking your boss on the journey with you.

You will need to take bold steps to forge a better bond with your boss and their peers. You may see some positive responses in the short term, but don't be surprised if it takes several months to build the kind of trust and rapport you want. This technique is very powerful, but it needs to become a way of life.

Here's to you building a more successful relationship with your boss!

PART THREE

THE PERSONAL
ENTREPRENEUR

9

Selling Yourself

- *Have you ever thought your CV may not quite be hitting the mark?*
- *Have you ever noticed your interviewer is not fully engaged in your interview?*
- *Do you feel that you may have missed some great job opportunities?*
- *Do you want to increase your chances of landing the 'right' job?*

To really impress recruiters, you need to create a knockout CV and give an outstanding interview, showing you understand and possess the key attributes the job requires.

Many things can damage a company's prospects such as a failure to anticipate and respond to changes in the market, governance-related fiascos that undermine its reputation and successful assaults on market share led by aggressive competitors. However, nothing is more pernicious and devastating than not recruiting the right people.

A company is a collection of skills deployed to achieve a goal. The most efficient companies deploy the right skills in the right places, without gaps or waste. Where skills are lacking—or in unnecessary abundance—efficiency suffers, and the company is weakened as a result. In fact, companies have failed because of a critical mismatch between skills and mission.

Companies face many risks, but this is by far the biggest and most potentially damaging, so it's no surprise that the best companies take recruitment extremely seriously, and the best leaders are laser-focused on getting the right people on their teams. When you aspire to join a company, you're seeking to be recognized as a great fit for its talent pool.

A great recruiter will test your claim without mercy. From the very first engagement with a potential employer, you must give the right impression. During the average recruitment process, you have two opportunities to shine—your application, supported by your CV, and if you're lucky enough to make the shortlist, your interview. We're going to look at both.

The Course of Your Life

Curriculum vitae is Latin for 'the course of your life'. Such an evocative phrase may seem overly grand for the purpose, but it carries an important message. A great CV is more than a simple rundown of what you've done and when. While an employer will want to know where you were educated and what experience you have, they are usually looking for much more. In fact, Alasdair once worked for a company that preferred to take no notice of education.

A knockout CV is a reflection of you on paper. It tells the reader the kind of person you are, the skills you've accumulated over your lifetime, and the way you perceive yourself. It indicates how you might react in key situations, giving a potential employer a sense of a fit far broader than a list of qualifications. If you want to be represented as professional, articulate and sharp, with depth and experience, it all needs to shine through in your CV.

Let's start with the basics. First, check your grammar and spelling. There are areas of professional life where precision in language is less important than others—legibility seems to be positively frowned upon in the medical profession, for instance! However, you aren't only trying to demonstrate your literacy here. If your CV isn't accurate and polished, you're casting doubt on your standards and ability right out of the gate. Care and attention to detail are indicators that you can be relied on at the most basic level, and the first place to reassure people you have these qualities is your CV.

A Knockout CV

Priyesh remembers an enthusiastic friend who worked in human resources, the department responsible for recruitment in any organization. He was French, with a passion for fine food—and a fine CV. He made it his mission to help Priyesh write a great CV early on in his career when he was applying for a job at an American investment bank. Priyesh got the job, and here are the key ingredients that went into that CV.

- Write your CV in reverse chronological order, with your most recent role at the top.
- Include a section on each firm you've worked for, including titles, roles and dates.
- Under each role, list snappy 'headline'—elevator pitch of sorts highlighting your achievements
- Begin each headline with an active verb that represents success in action.

Some examples of active verbs that you can use in your CV.

Delivered	Implemented	Achieved	Re-engineered	Optimized
Built	Established	Overhauled	Supervised	Enhanced
Led	Drove	Rolled out	Upgraded	Managed

Where possible, keep each achievement to one or two lines to demonstrate succinctness and clarity of thought. For example: 'Delivered a process re-engineering project, saving $1m in operating costs.' A dollar figure resonates with tangible benefits and draws the eye of time-constrained executives who are often screening hundreds of CVs.

Proven performance represented by measurable results is crucial for giving the right impression. If you're unable to assign measurable results to your achievements, you may want to take another look at what you're doing and refocus to become more tangible in your delivery—something that is likely to help you in your current role too.

In fact, writing a CV for yourself periodically is a great way to shine a light on your portfolio of achievement and provides an opportunity to assess your performance objectively, much like a prospective employer would.

Here's an example of a work experience section:

Excel Bank 2010–2015
Director (Risk), Global Head of Risk Operations (~200 team)
Re-engineered the Global Risk Data Platform
- Delivered a new big data analytics system to 3,000 users, reducing IT costs by $2m
- Built a team of 20 expert analysts in 6 months to support rollout of the new system
- Established a global data governance framework for data model review and control

When describing your current role, it's fine to include projects that are still underway. For example, you might say, 'Currently leading project to ....'

Where you have many achievements related to a project, try to group them together by theme, as shown in the example above: Re-engineered Global Risk Data Platform. You may have had multiple roles in an organization, so replicate this format for all your roles.

Be a Snowball, Not a Rolling Stone

Let your CV tell your story. A potential employer will try to see how you've built your strengths across your career. You need to articulate:

- How you built your profile. This can include your educational background and work experience.
- How you progressed. For example, by widening your experience or making a lateral move.
- How your experience has made you better at what you do.

Providing this thread of success demonstrates how you've gone from strength to strength throughout your career. It shows you that you aren't a rolling stone that gathers moss but rather, a snowball that takes on more and more substance as it travels along its journey.

You can do this by using similar language to describe each of your positions throughout your CV. That way, there will be little doubt that you're progressing by doing similar roles to a progressively higher level of seniority or applying that experience to different areas.

For example, your progression could look something like this:

- Financial control analyst
- Finance project manager
- IT project manager
- Finance programme manager

This narrative says you have a background in financial analysis and have used the knowledge you've gained at the ground level to run many successful projects. It's a great story of building depth and being rewarded for your successes, to the point where you're now trusted to deliver large-scale initiatives—maybe even independently. If you were applying for a job as a project manager in finance or IT, this trajectory would greatly improve your chances. However, even if you were applying for a project manager position in another department, you may still have a good chance, as your CV shows you have built and developed transferable skills.

Let's look at it another way. If you've jumped from job to job within a very short period of time, your CV will struggle to demonstrate any kind of professional depth. Clearly, it's best to avoid this situation, but if you're already there, aim to highlight common threads while leaning on the resulting breadth of your experience as the positive upshot.

Remember, you're selling yourself as a product and a service provider. People may want to buy a product that has many features, but they will want to focus on its core purpose first. You need to convince them you possess the skills and qualities they need. A car with a sunroof and surround sound system is nice, but it's of no use if it doesn't drive in a straight line.

If you are a project manager, analyst or salesperson, your experience, achievements and skills should demonstrate that you are—or are striving to become—the best in the business. Focus on that and tell your story as clearly as possible.

Synopsis

It's a good idea to provide a brief synopsis at the top of your CV. For example:

Global Operations Manager with 10 years' experience leading large teams, successfully delivering operational re-engineering and efficiency initiatives across two major banks. Seeking an opportunity to leverage and expand my operating model-optimization skills.

This is a good way of emphasizing certain aspects of your achievements, motivations and the kind of opportunity you are seeking, especially if you are aiming for a role where your experience may not present an obvious fit. However, on the flip side, an employer will expect you to have tailored your CV to the role you're applying for and will not simply take claims of a good fit at face value. Your synopsis should offer a high-level summary of four things:

1. Overall experience
2. Key areas of competence
3. Desired direction of travel
4. Skills and attributes you can bring to the job

These four points are essentially the foundation of what makes you worthy of being considered for the type of role you're looking for. However, don't be too specific—you don't want to inadvertently close the door on a great role by being too narrow in your outlook. Another word of caution: while it is important to emphasize relevant skills in your synopsis, it needs to be backed up by strong, succinct expressions of achievement in the main body of your CV.

Now that you have a great CV, go ahead and use it as a blueprint to plan a great interview. You may recall that we wrote headlines of achievements in our sample CV. Having done the same, you need to prepare a narrative for each of these achievements that fleshes out the story of your success. For each chapter of your story, include details like:

- How did you approach the task?
- What role did you play?
- How did you engage stakeholders?
- Did you lead or coordinate efforts?
- What excited you about this project?
- What did you learn from the experience?

Every line on your CV needs to be part of an engaging story about a project you completed, the approach you took and what you and your organization gained from it. Include positive experiences but also challenging situations, negotiations, examples of conflict management, project management and team motivation.

Interviewers will usually ask you to talk about a time when you:

- Dealt with a challenging situation
- Needed to motivate a team
- Negotiated with a difficult client or colleague
- Met a tight deadline
- Closed a major deal

Scan your history for situations that meet these criteria, so you have stories to tell when the question comes up. Consider where you can emphasize key characteristics and skills that are deemed important for the job you're interviewing for. Make sure you rehearse each story. This is the story of your career. You should know it inside out so you can speak about it with confidence, enthusiasm and fluency. That way, you'll come across as articulate and composed in the interview—key attributes for any high-performing employee.

Tell the Story

You should also practice putting the narrative of your whole career journey together, telling your story from your first job to your current one. Be ready to explain the thought process behind your decisions and detail two or three of your biggest achievements for each role. Alternatively, if you haven't been working for long, touch on all your achievements so far and prepare to pull out more details during the interview.

Demonstrate how you've gathered experience along the way and leveraged it as you've moved from role to role. As you advance through your career, think about how your next role could add to your CV, regardless of whether you plan to move companies in the future. After all, you need to be marketable within your existing company too.

When Priyesh was working as head of risk technology, he actively sought out a new opportunity to work with front-office trading systems, for the sole purpose of establishing a broad, end-to-end knowledge of investment banking technology. Today, he talks candidly about the logic behind the moves he made and demonstrates how they helped him develop his rich, detailed knowledge of investment banking systems.

It's also worth rehearsing your career story out of chronological order, as your interviewer could be interested in any part of your experience. Be confident of answers to questions about your expectations from your next role or typical questions like where you see yourself in five years' time.

Think of it as the next chapter of your career narrative, using the experience you've gained to move forwards and upwards. Provide a view that is ambitious but not impractical. As a project manager, you might say you see yourself managing large, global programmes but avoid saying you want to run the whole department, for example.

Dedicate plenty of time to researching the history, ethos and trajectory of the company you're interviewing at. You need a good answer to this question or one of its many variants: 'Why this company, and why now?'

You should develop a clear, logical progression of your career to date and an ambitious but practical vision of your possible future.

One final, golden rule—remember that for anything you've written on your CV, you need to demonstrate that you can explain it in depth.

A good interviewer will drill down into your career record and scrutinize each point. For example, they will be interested in:

- How much you really understand your current and past roles.
- Whether you have the intellectual curiosity to delve into the details.
- Your degree of knowledge and transferable skills.

So, be prepared to 'peel the onion' and go into detail about all aspects of your roles, past and present, using your achievement stories and other details. The more depth, insight and opinion you can bring to the table, the more you will come across as someone who is ready and willing to continue learning and growing within a role.

First Steps

If you're looking for your first job, you won't have a career full of achievements to dazzle your interviewer with. That said, you should still have some stories to tell. Here are a few examples.

- A university project like your dissertation (to showcase application, enthusiasm and intellect)
- Sporting achievements (to showcase teamwork and determination)
- A club you held a senior position in (to showcase leadership promise)

- Performance experience like music or theatre (to showcase dedication and breadth of interest)
- Volunteering or charity work (to showcase empathy and goodwill)

If you're a new graduate, front-load your CV with your educational achievements. Your time in education is likely far more substantial than your work history. Having said that, you may have some part-time work or internship experience under your belt. If you don't, however, we strongly encourage you to get some.

What employers look for in a graduate or post-graduate is raw potential. They want to see intellectual ability and the curiosity to learn, which you can demonstrate through good grades, interesting research projects and wide reading. Some employers will also use psychometric tests, either developed in-house or contracted out to a specialist firm. These vary greatly, but there are some standard approaches, and it is worth putting in some preparation.

Employers will also look for leadership, teamwork and organizational skills via membership in sports teams, debating societies and social clubs. Other highly prized soft skills include enthusiasm, which can come across in an interview; what a candidate has learnt; and what skills they are interested in attaining or enhancing going forward.

Finally, when interviewing for your first job, always remember, interviewers want to ensure that the interviewee is a good cultural fit for the firm. Friends and contacts who are familiar with the company will be able to give you a grounding in this tricky interview technique. The company website may also give pointers. Log on and soak it up like a sponge. Find out all the key facts about the company—history, strategy, market position, size and locations—to demonstrate a strong desire to be part of it. It is not always possible to gauge a firm's culture from the outside, so showing that you're flexible and willing to adapt is useful.

Even if you're applying for your first job, aim to build as strong a CV as you can—know your achievements and be prepared to tell your story with enthusiasm. Demonstrate intellectual curiosity with a strong desire to be part of an organization—and grow with it.

The Not-So-Subtle Steps

- Ensure your CV is immaculate with clear, consistent formatting and no typos.
- List the firms, roles and titles you've held, working backwards from your current role.
- List all your achievements as headlines, starting with active verbs such as 'delivered' that focus attention on tangible results.
- Include a synopsis at the top of your CV to summarize the key attributes of your career and what you are seeking from future opportunities.
- Demonstrate that you're a 'snowball', building your knowledge, ability and contributions as you move through your career.
- Rehearse detailed, real-life stories of your achievements. Keep in mind the generic questions interviewers often ask so you can refer to your experience where relevant.
- Paint a clear picture of your career journey, linking different roles with a logical thread and explaining what you're looking to gain in a new role.
- Be prepared to 'peel the onion' of what you've learnt and understood in your current role to demonstrate your intellectual curiosity.

- If you're applying for your first job, list your education first and give examples of achievements, leadership, teamwork, enthusiasm and adaptability.

As you can see, preparation is critical. If you're having trouble aligning your CV to the attributes required for the role you want, it could be you're not ready for it just yet. In that case, the preparation process will highlight where you need to focus to fill those gaps in your achievements and prepare for your next big move.

10

The Business of You

- *Do you feel like your career is stuck in one place?*
- *Would you like to accelerate your climb up the corporate ladder?*
- *Do you think you're ready for a promotion but someone else is more likely to get it?*
- *Do you need a helping hand with your career progression?*

Moving ahead in your career requires proving your worth, demonstrating achievement, and showing you're ready for the next level. To learn how to take that step, read on.

From the position of post room assistant to CEO, everyone reports to someone. In the post room, the manager is the top dog and will expect their team to meet the targets they set. Meanwhile, those pressurized quarterly meetings under the stern gaze of the board of directors are a reminder of the CEO's place in the corporate hierarchy—and the chair of the board probably feels the same when they face shareholders.

Everyone has someone to whom they answer in their professional life. When it comes to building your career, however, the person you're really working for is ... you.

You are the MD and CEO of your own corporation. If you want to earn business, then just like Amazon or Tesla, you need to dedicate yourself to serving your clients. In the same way Amazon strives to deliver the right items on time or Tesla strains corporate muscles to get top-of-the-line electric cars to its clients, you need to commit yourself to satisfying those who come to you for the services you promise.

Once you gain this perspective and start to see those around you as clients, you will find that your whole outlook on work changes. The business of you becomes a service provider to your clients, understanding what they really want—just as a company would—and making sure you deploy the right resources to fulfil their requirements.

This is more than simply pleasing your boss. Yes, your boss is a client, be they the post room manager or chair of the board, but this way of looking at things goes much further. Your colleagues, your employees and even the clients of the company you work for are all your clients too. In short, anyone who can affect your reputation and revenue is critical to the expansion of the business of you, and therefore, to your career progression.

The idea that you're at work to provide a service to your personal clients that helps them strengthen their reputation and generate a positive return is a powerful behavioural driver. When you meet your team, colleagues or boss, ask them, 'How can I help you?' Especially if they look like they may need a hand, you might even consider volunteering to support them. If they accept, think of it as winning new business for yourself. If they don't express any need for support at the moment, at least you've created a positive feeling and sown a seed for next time, when perhaps they will need your assistance.

If someone comes to you for support, look at it as a fabulous opportunity to build a positive relationship and do your utmost to help. You may only be able to provide partial support—perhaps advice or an introduction to someone in a better position to help than you—but it will go a long way just the same. If you do agree to help, ensure you fulfil your commitment. If you're asked for something you don't believe you can deliver, respectfully decline and give a clear reason why. Perhaps you have conflicting priorities, or the request draws on skills you haven't yet developed.

Building a reputation for being helpful, productive and approachable will increase the likelihood that people seek you out when they need support. Think about it—if you were racing to meet a deadline or juggling competing tasks, who would you go to for help? You would look for someone you knew to be both willing and reliable. Make sure you're that person. Cultivating an attitude of being in service to your colleagues keeps you humble and will win the hearts and minds of your colleagues, clients and bosses.

Build Depth: Be Outstanding

Every business thrives or fails depending on the quality of its products. People remain loyal to good products. They recommend them to their friends. They trust the producer and will favour their new products over those of competitors. The business of you is no different. To win the loyalty of your clients, you should aim to be outstanding at your core job.

If you're a project manager, aim to be the best project manager you can be by ensuring the following:

- Know the latest planning standards
- Take pride in your project materials
- Be prepared to work all hours to ensure you deliver

And just as great companies do, take full accountability for your product and your deliverables. That's how you cement trust in you and in your ability. A successful engagement delivering high-quality, positive outcomes acts as a springboard to win more assignments. Gradually, as you prove you can achieve results, you will find you're given more responsibility, and your reputation will grow.

In the business world, notoriety as someone who can be trusted to meet their commitments is the single most important accelerator for rising up the corporate ladder. It's been a key element in our success too. When we are asked to make something happen and we commit to it, we deliver without fail and to the highest possible quality.

However, to progress in your career, this has to mean more than excelling in your core role. When it comes to taking the next step, achieving excellence in your previous position isn't enough. If you want to be recognized as a good fit for a more senior role, you must demonstrate abilities beyond your current job description.

That doesn't mean you need to be an expert at everything right from the start. However, it does mean you'll have to work hard to demonstrate an understanding of the challenges associated with a new task and the skills required to overcome it; that you will learn enough—and maybe a little more—to explain the logic behind the approach you choose. Then, of course, you must pass the ultimate test: successful completion of the task.

Aim to build a degree of expertise in every key task you're given, commit to deliver an outstanding product, own the outcome and look forward to more responsibility.

Solve a Big Problem

Clients know a successful business when they see one, which is exactly why they remain clients and recommend those businesses to others. You want to be noticed and commended just like those businesses, so do something commendable!

The quickest route to commendation is to help solve a significant problem for your boss, department or organization. It might mean working with or winning over a difficult client, cracking a complex analysis problem or delivering a time-critical project. Throughout our careers, we've shown enthusiasm for taking on projects that others were reluctant to tackle—and reaped the rewards too.

In 2006, Priyesh wanted to gain experience in the front office of the investment bank he was working for. It is the revenue-generating part of the bank where the multi-million—sometimes multi-billion-pound—deal-makers, traders and bankers help big corporations manage their finances. It sounded like an exciting place to work—at the cutting edge of business strategy and brimming with clever, ambitious people who thrive under pressure.

Priyesh primarily wanted this experience so he could be a more effective partner to a part of the organization that is often seen as aggressive and intimidating. It would give him a fully rounded, front-to-back experience of the company's entire transactional process, from deal-making to trading to settlement with clients, as well as accounting and risk management.

It was a big professional leap. He was some way into his career working with middle-office technology where the bank's accounting and risk management systems live. His opportunity came when he discovered through his internal network that senior management wanted to develop a new trading platform to expand their oil trading business—and to catch a high tide in the market, they needed it fast. Success would add millions to the bottom line. This sounded like a perfect opportunity for Priyesh.

The drawback was that it came with a near-impossible deadline of eight months. Not only that, the project would be under intense scrutiny from the bank's management board. So, while the prize for success was great, failure or delay could spell the end of his career at the bank. He picked up the gauntlet and, applying strong project risk management strategy, delivered to target. The positive result was celebrated by the firm, and his boss widened his field of responsibility to manage the entire trading IT platform. We talk more about the techniques he applied in Chapter 12, 'The View from the Corner Office'.

While delivering on your current tasks, keep an eye out for those big challenges. Be a great problem-solver. Be bold and take calculated risks—the rewards will come.

Support Success

Success is contagious. If you can support someone and help them gain success, your star will rise along with theirs. Do not fall into the trap of thinking that you'll somehow diminish yourself by supporting someone else. As I've already said, being helpful helps you in the long run.

Align yourself wisely. Look out for colleagues who are aiming to solve a key issue, deliver something spectacular and help your organization achieve its ambitions. Support people who are looking to make a material difference to the success of the business. It could be your boss, a colleague or a client. Regardless, it's an opportunity to complement your normal job by engaging in a special initiative. Consider offering to support something designed to improve your firm's bottom line. Put in extra effort outside the scope and hours of your normal work to support the leader on a challenging project.

For the business of you, as with any business, the guiding principle should be getting a good return on your investment (ROI)—ensuring that you get enough benefit out of your extracurricular project to justify the effort and risk. Putting maximum effort into an initiative the firm greatly values will deliver higher returns than an activity that's low down on the list of priorities. That isn't to say you ignore the more mundane tasks, but when prioritizing, save the big personal sacrifices for results the firm deems critical and is actively promoting.

The rewards may not be immediate, but that doesn't necessarily make them less valuable. If you support an individual as they strive for success, you will often find you have built a strong alliance for life. We've both been incredibly fortunate to work with superiors and clients who had ambitious visions that we helped make into a reality. If you can back someone's dream, you form a lifelong professional partnership built on trust and, as you deliver together, you can build longstanding friendships too.

People talk about work–life balance, but there isn't a clear division between work and life. The two blend into one another, so it's important to make sure that the time you spend at work is time you consider valuable in the context of your life. Friendships that begin at work will usually transcend the company you work for. They will follow you as you move to new jobs and become part of your daily life. Opportunities of this kind do not come along every day, but when they do, grab them—even if it means working harder or taking more risks.

Ask for It, Prove It, Move Up

Sometimes, things come to us out of the blue. Opportunities present themselves with no warning and little work on our part. These chances are rare, and if we rely on fate to deliver our next role to us on a silver platter, we may be waiting a very long time. Usually, we have to fight tooth-and-nail for such opportunities. If you know you can do more, are confident in your ability and are willing to take some risk, you should let people know you want to be considered for something more involved. Even if they can't satisfy your ambition immediately, they're more likely to bear you in mind when circumstances change.

If there is ever any doubt about your readiness for a new challenge, use this formula:

- Ask for the responsibility, even as a trial.
- Deliver success.
- Become established in the role.

Early on in his career, Priyesh was working as a project manager for a US investment bank and had enjoyed a reasonable amount of success. At that time, a major programme was veering off course. The project was to rebuild a complex system that supported the daily profit-and-loss calculations for a multi-million-dollar trading business that had outgrown it. It had become bogged down and needed fresh impetus and discipline. Priyesh was sent in to help turn it around, and he was making good headway.

At the same time, the organization was looking for someone to head the whole business area. Priyesh plucked up the courage to ask his boss for the management role and laid out the strategy he would put in place if he got the job. His boss was supportive, but he was also concerned that his MD might not want to take a risk with a junior, given how important the project was. Priyesh organized a meeting with the MD, an extremely clever and friendly Irishman. He repeated his request and set out the reasons why he thought he should be trusted with the responsibility. He spoke about his solid track record with this project and the ones he'd handled previously and outlined the approach he proposed to take. He readily drew on the support of his boss too.

The MD was swayed, and Priyesh was given the position. The project was no walk in the park. It required a focus on every aspect of delivery. Priyesh revised the scope into sensible chunks so the team could see tangible progress quicker and easier. He worked closely with clients, so they felt fully engaged. He brainstormed complex technical problems with experts and reported challenges and achievements clearly and openly. He sacrificed time to prove he could make this a success, going to great lengths to find a solution for every challenge and showing the team was in control and open to advice. The success of this project resulted in his promotion to the next level.

If you think you can take on more responsibility and are ready to help solve a problem for your organization, do not be afraid to ask for the opportunity. Even if your managers think this isn't your time, you've let them know that you're eager to serve on a larger scale. When the next opportunity comes along, they may think of you. You don't need to sit back and wait. Ask for feedback on why you weren't selected and learn from it to raise your chances of being considered for the next opening. When you're given a chance, grab it with both hands and over-deliver to prove to your superiors that they made the right choice.

Be the Promotion You Want

So, you're successful in your role and you've taken on extra challenges, demonstrating your willingness to go further and your ability to deliver. However, taking on more senior roles involves more than desire, hard work and a proven track record. You need to show you know what that higher level of responsibility entails in terms of behaviour.

Here's a great rule of thumb—if you want to be promoted, start mentally operating at the next level. That doesn't mean doing the job you're seeking or acting as if you've already been promoted. It means thinking yourself into the mode of operation that goes with the role. Notice how people at the next level operate:

- How do they approach challenges?
- How do they communicate?
- What makes them stand out?
- What do you respect about them?
- How are they different from you?
- How does their behaviour differ from yours?

It's important to choose the right people. Pick out high-performing employees and compare yourself to them. There's no point setting your benchmark at the bottom. Consider whether you can request for one of them to be your mentor. Many companies have formal mentoring arrangements, where the HR department matches mentors with mentees. Even if your company doesn't offer this or the suggested mentor isn't someone you've chosen, you can approach people informally to ask for guidance. Most people will accept a call for help. Remember, it's quite flattering when someone asks you to teach them what you know.

When approaching someone for mentoring, lay out some ground rules before you start. A general appeal to 'tell me where I'm going wrong' is unlikely to draw the kind of specific guidance you need. It may end up giving the impression you're less sophisticated in your self-reflection than you actually are. Identify areas where your prospective mentor excels, or areas where you consider yourself to be lacking.

It may be that you're not building relationships with colleagues and senior staff that you'd like to have but can see another individual navigating these difficult waters with ease. Perhaps your nerves let you down when you present to senior colleagues, and you aspire to be like another employee who can hold a room and deliver their message with confidence. When searching for help, focusing on a niche like this will make the mentoring process more fruitful and efficient for both of you. Of course, if someone proves themselves to be a particularly effective mentor, you can always go back for more!

We've benefitted from great mentorship, both by observing seniors and asking for advice after we established a degree of rapport. Mostly, it's about seeking help to reach the next stage in your career. Sometimes, it's most effective to work back from a five-year target and request advice from a senior on the best path.

Both of us have also mentored junior colleagues and friends. Priyesh has helped budding politicians with their election speeches and consultants who wanted to become partners. Meanwhile, Alasdair has mentored colleagues on the principles of crafting a successful career. We both see it as a duty and a critical part of our role to mentor others and help them reach their full potential. This book is an embodiment of that desire to share some of what we've learnt ourselves from great mentors, coaches and leaders.

A word of caution here. Just as you're looking for guidance and support from senior colleagues, your peers and junior look up to you for support. Do not let arrogance creep into your approach. Confidence, assertiveness and enthusiasm to deliver are the right attributes to magnify but don't forget to continue serving your peers. After all, sincere service is a key selling point for the business of you, and you'll need all the well-wishers you can get to support your next move.

Finally, as well as your peers, it's essential that you can also count on your boss and some of their peers to support you. There are more tips on how to build a strong relationship with your boss and their peers in Chapter 7, 'Building a Network'.

Choose the Right Path

Not all routes upwards lead to the top. Some may look promising but prove too steep to climb. Sometimes, we find we aren't progressing in our career as quickly as we'd like, and we struggle to understand why. Is it because there's a glass ceiling stopping us from climbing the ladder? Is it because we've hit our limits and lack the capacity to go further? Perhaps we've failed to make the right impression on those around us.

These are all possibilities, but there is another problem that can be hard to recognize and acknowledge. Perhaps we are on the wrong path and, try as we might, this route is not going to bring us to the destination we seek. Ambition can blind us, while recognizing that we need to reassess our aspirations can be painful.

Pushing on and just trying harder only results in wasted effort if it turns out we're on the wrong path. In these circumstances, we will only progress if we recognize the position we're in and do something to change it. In practice, this probably means looking for a sideways move into an arena where we can better leverage our skills. It might mean leaving our employer and working for someone else, but not necessarily.

The perfect opportunity may be in another department or team where your skills are in greater demand. It could also be that there simply isn't any room for growth in your current department. Perhaps there's only one senior role available at the next level and that belongs to your boss, who shows no intention of going anywhere soon.

Priyesh was the deputy chief operating officer for the IT department of a major investment bank, with a designation of vice president. He wanted to move up to a full-fledged COO, a director-level position. He'd been in the job for two years and achieved some noted successes, but the organization didn't think he was ready to take the next step. They felt he needed more practical project management experience in the technology field. He realized that was experience he simply wasn't going to get in his current role, so he asked his boss to sanction him the ability to explore opportunities elsewhere in the organization.

Priyesh had built up a good reputation in the IT department, and a leader in risk technology gave him an opportunity to join their team as a project manager. He worked incredibly hard to make this role a success and won a promotion to head of market risk technology. After successfully delivering several projects, he was promoted to director. Five years later, he moved into a role as COO for market risk. It took a while, but if he hadn't made that sideways move, five years could have gone by, and he would have been no better off.

Similarly, Alasdair was working for a major publishing organization as a specialist in Latin America, where he'd cut his teeth as a foreign correspondent. He envisioned a bright future with this organization, but opportunities for advancement were limited. The editorial team was organized regionally, and regional head was the most senior role he could aspire to without leaving his professional roots behind.

So, when an opportunity came up to lead an initiative with a global focus, he embraced it with enthusiasm. The first challenge was to persuade his employers that he could make the leap from a relatively narrow regional focus to a worldwide brief—something he'd already had to convince himself of at that point. He quickly discovered that the curiosity and analytical skills he had used so far served him equally well in his new role while taking on a young project and spreading his geographical wings opened up new fields of opportunity.

We're not recommending you simply jump ship and change roles when the going gets tough—that's unlikely to win you a promotion. We're saying you need to be honest with yourself and recognize when you're in a position where you need to gain a different type of experience to advance to the next level. Leaving an organization solely in the hope that your next employer will promote you is a bad idea. It would be strange to win a promotion in a new organization when an employer that knows you doesn't believe you have the requisite skills.

If you're motivated to move on because there's no prospect of a suitable vacancy arising at your current organization, you may need to take a step back in your new organization to rebuild your connections and reputation. If you do get offered a promotion, be sure you understand the risk you're taking and be honest with yourself. Does this new role demand skills you haven't yet developed? While that's not a reason to rule it out, beware—it's tough to take on a new role and really hit the ground running if you're having to learn the skills required to do it. Of course, the risk may well be worth the return, but it is a risk.

If you've nurtured your connections in your existing role, you should use them to seek the advice of those senior to you—either your immediate boss or other experienced leaders. Their feedback could be invaluable. You should certainly do this before rushing to leave. They may be able to offer advice on opportunities to consider in your organization or indicate whether hard work and persistence are likely to pay off down the line.

The Not-So-Subtle Steps

- Develop an awareness that you work for yourself. You're running your own business and it is only by serving your organization, team, peers, clients and boss that you will earn more business. Be of service and build a strong reputation for being useful.

- Be outstanding at your job. Build depth of knowledge and expertise. Super-specialize in your role. Prove that you can learn quickly and win a reputation for delivery-without-fail to demonstrate you can be trusted with new challenges.
  Look for an opportunity to solve a big problem for your organization. Be bold and prepared to take a calculated risk. If you succeed, it will strengthen your reputation as an achiever. Even if you fail, you may well gain respect.
- Support a rising star or strong performer to be even more successful.
- Invest extra time and effort in an initiative that's critical for the firm.
- If you think you're ready for the next big opportunity, ask for it. If you're lucky enough to be given a chance, put your heart and soul into it.
- Observe, learn and adopt the positive attributes of leaders operating above you. Model yourself on high performers and be honest about the skills you need to develop. Continue to respect your team, peers and bosses to retain their support.
- Are you definitely on the right path? Ensure there isn't a significant skill, experience or opportunity gap hindering your progression. If there is, try to bridge it and seek internal advice before you consider jumping ship to another organization.
- If you do consider an external move, make sure it represents a real opportunity to grow and be aware that you will probably be working harder than ever.

11

Married to the Job: The Role of HR

- *How much do you know about the role of human resources (HR)?*
- *Why is HR important to you as a leader?*
- *Do you know how you can help HR to help you succeed?*

The HR department is critical for the smooth functioning of an organization, but it is also key to your personal advancement throughout your career. Working effectively with the HR can help you make the right choices in your professional life.

When people say someone is married to their work, it's rarely a compliment. Being too committed to one's work is seen as damaging to other aspects of your life—your actual marriage for instance. The term 'workaholic' expresses it nicely: dangerously addicted to your professional role, to the detriment of all other relationships. There is a certain gung-ho bravado around workaholics, but few would truly want to be one.

There's another way of looking at it. 'Married to the job' doesn't have to mean 'divorced from life'. Indeed, the best marriages make life better. Each partner is made happier by their association with the other, and the relationship brings deeper satisfaction than either partner could experience alone. A great marriage isn't a hermetic relationship that eschews all other aspects of life. It is a willing partnership that affords both sides a happier existence.

In seeking this type of ideal relationship with your career, you have a key ally—the HR department. Much maligned, popularly dismissed as form-fillers and rule enforcers, dubbed 'Human Remains' by office humourists, HR gets a rough deal, but these characterizations are far from the truth. HR specialists are facilitators of your relationship with the organization; they are there to support you throughout your career.

To extend the marriage metaphor, the role of HR is to ensure that you and the firm are lawfully wedded, for better or worse, richer or poorer, in sickness and in health, until death—or a better job—do you part.

Lawfully Wedded

When you join an organization, it is important you fully understand the terms of your contract. Although most of it isn't up for negotiation, HR is critical in ensuring you understand the options, benefits and boundaries of your job. If an HR specialist is present at the interview, it's a great way to get a clear understanding of what you're signing up for.

Without making it an interrogation, it's reasonable to ask HR to clarify points that may not be obvious from the job advertisement. For instance, are there any non-salary benefits offered such as a gym membership, health schemes or subsidized transport?

Alasdair remembers how the introduction of a structured training programme improved morale among employees and offered an incentive to candidates in a competitive labour market. The programme covered languages, economics and other areas relevant to the job. HR will know this kind of thing chapter-and-verse, and it can make a real difference when you're deciding where you want to work.

Remember, the interview is a key opportunity for you to boost your package beyond what's initially on offer; after all, you may not get another one for a while.

Ask the HR specialist about the culture of the organization:

- How does it support internal mobility?
- What sort of training and development initiatives are available?
- Does the firm support any internal clubs or associations?
- Is there a mentoring scheme in operation?
- Is there a culture of proactive personal development?
- Will the company help you set long-term goals and support you in achieving them?
- Does the company permit flexible working, such as working from home if needed?

HR specialists are experts in this area and best placed to explain them to you. They will also appreciate the interest you show in the organization. Joining a choir may seem a marginal activity for an IT operative, but a narrow focus on the immediate demands of the job description is unlikely to inspire either you or your employer.

It is important to gauge the culture of an organization. You're potentially making a long-term investment in joining a company. You need to feel comfortable or at least know the rules of the road. There are few circumstances where you would want to marry a stranger, so before you become lawfully wedded to your firm, ensure you thoroughly understand your contract and have a sense of what it's like to be employed by this organization.

Remember, the HR specialist is also interviewing you, so it's important you make a good impression during the exchange. Chapter 9, 'Sell Yourself', has plenty more on that.

For Better, for Worse

In a dynamic environment like a medium or large corporation, there are bound to be ups and downs. During the ups, HR will be your adviser, facilitator and cheerleader. During the downs, they will be your marriage counsellor.

HR specialists are usually involved in discussions around promotions and pay rises. Their expertise helps to ensure that rewards are in line with those enjoyed by employees of similar skill levels, as well as your personal performance and company policy.

Remember, your salary comes out of the same pot as everyone else's, and companies often have to make difficult decisions about how that pot is distributed. In other words, you won't always get what you think you are worth, but that may not be because the company doesn't value you. While looking for recognition, it is worth bearing in mind, the opinion of your HR partner is highly valued by other decision-makers.

Good HR partners are well-trained in understanding an individual's strengths and weaknesses as a leader, so they can be great allies on your professional development journey. They can identify the right training courses for you, and many are great coaches themselves. Their advice on how to progress can be highly valuable, but the department is usually stretched incredibly thin, so make any time you can get with them count.

When things aren't going well—perhaps you're not getting on with a colleague or you're struggling to meet your commitments—your first point of call should be your manager. They will try to resolve the situation if you can't do anything about it yourself, but sometimes, the situation is more delicate. Maybe it's your manager you're not getting on with. In these cases, seeking advice directly from HR may be a better idea.

In all your dealings with HR, it's important to remember that the department also works for the firm. While they have a duty of care to you, they are also there to protect the company's interests, so avoid bringing minor matters to them. Not only is it a waste of their time, but it also suggests you may not be a good leader or able to handle challenges on your own.

Help them to help you by being factual, constructive and supportive of the firm, while being honest about how the situation is affecting you. Professional difficulties can be emotional, but it's best to set emotions aside and focus on how your work, productivity and progress are being affected. There's more on this in Chapter 4, 'Control Your Emotions'. If you're unsure, it's better to approach HR off the record than to raise a formal grievance. They may be able to help you resolve the situation discreetly, while an official complaint automatically triggers a sequence of events that may be more disruptive than the case merits.

If you have a minor issue with an employee, it's usually best to resolve it directly with them if you can. If things start to escalate beyond your control, the HR department is always there to help. In the worst circumstances, HR specialists can be invaluable advisers on the fairest approach to take, both for the individual concerned and the firm.

It is at times like these that the HR discipline really comes into its own for most staff members. Work closely with them, follow their advice, and give your honest perspective, and together, you can find the right solution for the firm and the employee.

For Richer, for Poorer

Remember, your manager is also likely to be knowledgeable on HR matters and will probably be able to answer most questions related to pay and allowances. After all, they need the same knowledge themselves.

One of the roles HR play that your manager cannot is to advise the firm on whether it is competitive in the labour market in terms of what it pays its employees. HR specialists will usually start this process by acquiring surveys from the market to understand pay trends.

It is not usually advisable to raise a formal point with HR on pay. It is the responsibility of your boss to decide your compensation based on your performance. However, if you believe the firm is paying under the market rate and you have evidence, providing this information to HR can help them with analysis and benchmarking.

Alasdair remembers dealing with a member of his team who insisted for some time that they were under-compensated by the firm for the duties they carried out. Informal discussions weren't enough to resolve the question, and, in the end, Alasdair requested a formal benchmarking exercise from the company's HR department.

Confronted with HR's judgement that their salary was indeed in line with similarly skilled individuals working for other firms, the team member accepted the position. They continued to press for higher compensation, which they were quite within their rights to do, but no longer argued that the firm was undervaluing them relative to others in the market.

If the benchmarking exercise had supported the team member's case, the company would have been in a tricky position with its existing salary structure, with implications for its overall budget. The evidence gathered by the HR department and its ability to act as an intermediary between the employee and the firm brought the issue to a conclusion all could agree with. Even if the employee was no better off, their grievance was resolved and, with Alasdair's help, they were able to focus on other factors that were holding them back.

So, if you feel you are being paid less than the fair market rate, first raise it with your manager. While you can mention it to an HR specialist, they may just be one input in the calculations of your manager and those further up the hierarchy.

Of course, the best way to achieve higher rewards is to perform well. Companies hate to lose great employees—assets they may have invested in over a long period of time—and will often compete to hold on to them. That usually means a larger salary or a more senior role. Great leaders know their value and aren't afraid to respectfully make their bosses aware of it. However, while loyalty to a firm may mean less dramatic increases in pay than moving from one firm to another, it comes with its own rewards.

While your employer will want to be sure you're being paid a fair wage, it is impossible to keep all employees rigidly in line with the market all the time. There are other drains on the firm's resources that may take precedence, depending on its overall performance. If you shine in a firm going through a difficult patch, your salary may lag behind that of a less impressive employee with a company in a better market position. However, that situation may reverse when things improve. Before going to war over pay, consider how far below the market you think you are and trade it off against the cost of moving to another firm.

Think about giving up the network you've built within the firm and the reputation and goodwill you've accumulated. If you really give it some thought, you may judge these things are worth more than the extra money you could earn elsewhere.

In Sickness and in Health

Your work life is about much more than money. The average person spends more than 90,000 hours of their life at work, and they are often the most demanding hours of the day. It's no surprise that working conditions can have a huge impact on our health and well-being.

Generally, day-to-day health matters aren't an issue for HR unless they're having a big impact on your work. You should look to raise issues with your boss first and let them advise HR as required. That said, there is a very fine line between concerns you can deal with yourself, those that belong with your boss, and more serious issues that require the kind of formal procedure for which HR is best suited.

You may be reluctant to go public with a health concern because you feel it will reflect on your ability to perform in your job or damage your prospects of promotion. On rare occasions, this can be the case, but far more often, the reluctance to share concerns ends up with those concerns going unresolved and becoming exacerbated.

In the pressurized environment of a busy company, it's natural for stress to build up. Chapter 4: Controlling Your Emotions offers some useful guidance but be aware too that many senior managers are trained to understand the toll that stress can take. Many will know it first-hand, and they are trained to handle such issues with care.

If the burden of work is getting too much, it's best to tell your manager. They may be able to reduce your workload or give you some guidance on stress management. Alasdair has rearranged employee schedules on numerous occasions in response to appeals from over-stretched team members. Sometimes, the sense you have an ally in your corner who truly has your back can help to dissipate some of the stress you're experiencing.

While your manager can offer a friendly ear and practical solutions, HR will usually be able to provide more structured support. First, they will be able to confirm the company's rules and policies when it comes to issues like illness, bereavement, childcare, or workplace stress. There may be help available that your boss is unaware of or unable to authorize.

HR will also maintain a database of outside help they can refer you to such as mindfulness sessions. The trust you've built up with your HR partners means you can rely on them to deal with any issue in confidence, without letting it spill over and potentially affecting the company's judgement of your professional capabilities.

Till Death Do Us Part

Okay, this sounds more dramatic than it should, but for the sake of the metaphor, let's go with it. What we're really talking about is moving jobs. Be it through mutual agreement or a messy divorce, the termination of your employment with a company can be complicated. HR has a key role in easing the split and ensuring both sides leave on the best terms.

One of HR's common responsibilities is to conduct what is known as an exit interview to capture the reasons why you're leaving. While this is an opportunity to unload all your grievances, there are good reasons to keep the feedback constructive, factual, short and free of emotion. Avoid pointing fingers at people who wronged you and refer instead to the fantastic career opportunity you're pursuing. If there are genuine recommendations you can offer to help the firm develop, this is a good forum to do so, but keep it as depersonalized and constructive as you possibly can. It's the most civil and mature way to behave, but it is also a practical step given the relatively small size of the professional world most of us operate in. Both Priyesh and Alasdair have found themselves working with previous employers at various points in their careers. Both recommend maintaining a healthy relationship with a firm on the way out so you can continue to work together if you meet again further down the road.

Bear in mind, grudges are costly to bear in terms of your own well-being, and they can stop you enjoying the many benefits you can get out of any period of employment. Future employers will want good references, and they're more likely to be forthcoming from former colleagues who remember you fondly. It's always good to keep in touch with colleagues and remain an active member of the firm's alumni network. The marriage may have ended, but that's no need to let that stop you seeing the kids!

The Not-So-Subtle Steps

If people spent more time with marriage counsellors when things are going well, the divorce rate would probably be a lot lower. Similarly, your partners in HR can help accelerate your career both in the good times and the challenging ones. From today onwards, keep the importance of your HR colleagues firmly in your mind:

- When starting a new role, work with HR specialists to fully understand the contractual terms and seek their advice on benefit options and culture.
- Remember, HR can provide development advice. Their opinion is valued when promotions and pay rises are being considered.

- Employees should address any problems with their direct manager. If that's not an option, HR can ensure the right approach is taken for the employee and the firm.
- Compensation discussions should be had with your manager. However, there are times when providing general information about compensation trends can be useful to HR and may ultimately benefit the firm in recalibrating its pay scales.
- Report any health issues affecting your work to your manager, who can inform HR. If a health concern becomes unbearable, raise it with your manager or HR.
- When leaving a firm, provide constructive, non-emotional, factual feedback to HR in your exit interview. You may wind up working with the firm again in the future.

Good luck building a relationship with your internal ally and counsellor.

PART FOUR

JOURNEY'S END, JOURNEY'S BEGINNING

12

The View from the Corner Office

Congratulations! Hard work and good decisions have taken you to the proverbial corner office. Look at that view—isn't it awesome? But now isn't the time to relax. You came here because you knew that given the opportunity, you would leave a mark. For that, you're going to have to do a lot more work and learn many more lessons.

We use the concept of the corner office—actual or virtual—as a privileged location from which you can survey the landscape you've left behind and enjoy the fruits of your success. But that's not quite how it works in real life. We've talked a lot about the benefits of providing service to those around us, learning from those further along our desired career path, and winning the respect and recognition of individuals who can further our careers.

Now that we have achieved seniority—maybe even a seat on the management committee or the board of directors—there's a shift in balance. Duty and responsibility are as important as ever, but now, we dedicate them to the service of the organization, its clients, and our colleagues, peers and juniors. In short, the emphasis now is on leadership.

What does it mean to be a leader? Well, a collection of all the books on the subject would easily pack the Library of Congress to the rafters, but it's worth going back to the simplest of definitions. For all the guru guides, business school lore and management theory, it boils down to this—a leader is followed. From that simple description, many things flow. If nobody follows, you're not leading. If people do what they do because you instruct them to, they are obeying, not following. You may be an excellent manager, but you're not a leader.

And you haven't come all this way to be a manager.

Our history is festooned with fine leaders, from Alexander the Great to Winston Churchill, and it wouldn't be trite to suggest studying them, but ultimately, you will be better off looking closer to home. The best examples are the ones who, when your long journey to the corner office is over and you look back, you realize you've respected, emulated and followed during key periods of your career. These are personal examples who inspired and supported you and without whom, you might not have made it.

Eastern spiritualism teaches that by carefully observing a master, you can acquire their prowess. Having worked for twenty years across industry-leading companies, we've had the good fortune to work with and learn from some of the best managing directors around. Although each is unique in their own way, they share many common traits that support and accentuate their effectiveness—and were probably key rungs on their own career ladders.

The following traits, though not exhaustive, describe several of the most effective leadership tools at our disposal. Some of the leaders we've observed may focus on certain traits more than others, but most apply them selectively as circumstances require.

Trait One: Riding the Wave

Managing directors are agents of change. Their primary responsibility is to understand the big challenges facing their organization, devise a strategy to confront those challenges and make sure the right people and processes are in place to pursue it. They recognize that no company can stay successful without change. Rivals eat up a competitive advantage, and clients develop new preferences and expectations. Waves of change wash through entire industries, sweeping away those who fail to adapt in a process that Austrian-American economist Joseph Schumpeter called 'creative destruction'.

Bold, innovative managing directors may bring the energy and vision to create a wave of change on their own; after all, it has to come from somewhere. Look at some of today's champions of industry—Facebook's Mark Zuckerberg, Amazon's Jeff Bezos and Tesla's Elon Musk are fine examples. However, for all the headlines they garner, such cases are rare.

Most good managing directors succeed because they recognize the wave currently driving change in their industry—which is very different from pursuing change for the sake of change. It's all too common for incoming managing directors to become seduced by a desire to make a mark. They restructure divisions, promote favourites and sideline others. They set unfeasibly ambitious financial targets, call it 'stretching', and consider this a strategy. This is bluster, not leadership, and such individuals succeed through luck rather than design.

True leaders understand their company's position within the market and recognize the barriers to greater success. They will plot a strategy that overcomes those hurdles and gives the business its best chance of developing and holding a competitive advantage, and in doing so, communicate this vision clearly to their staff. Once a strategic direction has been agreed upon, they will apply the discipline that keeps every part of the company in proper alignment so the strategy can be delivered. It becomes part of their very existence.

'Schnell, Schnell, Schnell'—speed, speed, speed. That was the watchword of Deutsche bank spokesperson Rolf Breuer, characterizing his institution's merger with Bankers Trust. Priyesh, as a junior vice president who, along with many others at Bankers Trust, had heard about plans to cut 20,000 jobs, was contemplating making a speedy exit. Recognizing the mood, the bank's managing director walked the floor and gathered the team for an impromptu fireside chat. His rallying call went along the lines of:

> I know what you're all feeling, that some of you are probably thinking of leaving. I'm going to see this through. We're about to create the world's largest financial institution by market capital, and I'm convinced it's going to create exciting opportunities for us. I know some of you are worried because the press says we're being taken over, that this isn't a merger of equals, but I believe the best people will be given opportunities here. So, I'm asking everyone to put their best foot forward and help drive the merger. I believe we have the strongest team and systems, and I think that will be recognized.

This was enough for Priyesh and his department. This leader not only rode the wave of change, but he also encouraged his team to take the driving seat wherever they had the opportunity. As a result, the department was one of the few Bankers Trust chose to lead the Deutsche Bank team following the merger.

Trait Two: Courage to Take Risks

Most successful businesses—and a few unlucky failures—understand how to calculate the risks associated with any course of action and balance them against the rewards on offer. Where the reward isn't worth the risk, companies usually change course. Where risks are high but the reward is higher, companies will protect themselves against said risks and reach for the opportunity. Some fail, but they simply absorb the loss and move on.

This willingness to balance risk and reward works at a personal level too. Managing directors who transform organizations often choose to risk their professional reputation in service to the company's overarching strategy. The difference is that, while organizations use systematic methods to protect themselves against measurable risks, a leader often puts their neck on the line to deliver what's right for the firm without a safety net. While this takes courage, the upside for the firm—and therefore, for the leader—often justifies it. On the flip side, if the potential return is minimal, effective leaders will have the courage to drive their teams to either minimize risk or avoid it altogether.

Following the financial crisis, regulators were determined to review banking practices and recommend enhancements, particularly regarding the risk management processes that had so spectacularly failed to foresee or ward off the threat. Under the resulting avalanche of new regulations, banks were asked to develop their risk management departments and invest millions in new processes, systems and calculation models, all while they were recovering from the substantial losses they and their clients had suffered.

Against this background, a leader emerged in one of the major European banks. While he understood the technicalities of these new rules and the reasons why they were being imposed, he chose not to simply comply. Instead, he took a step back and proposed how a more flexible approach to risk management could not only meet the new standards but also drive a culture of enhanced risk management awareness, accountability and responsibility, from the front office right through to the back.

The vision clarified the roles, controls and best risk practices required of each major part of the bank and took a systematic approach to correct shortcomings. The strategy was presented to the management board, and each board member was asked to take personal accountability for their area. They would be given performance metrics at periodic meetings where they could assess themselves and be answerable to the board. The prize was a possibility that the regulator might recognize good practice and reward it by reducing the bank's regulatory capital requirements, which is the money a bank needs to set aside for a rainy day.

It was certainly a courageous move. After all, consider the complexity of a major investment bank—there are dozens of trading systems, thousands of traders and various computer algorithms executing around 1.5 million trades a day. There are more than 20,000 people involved in post-processing those trades, with hundreds of data feeds flowing from the front office to the back through countless systems and spreadsheets and even via manual entry and adjustments. The prize depended on the ability to demonstrate with a high degree of confidence that the bank understood and was managing all the risk involved in these trades. Think of it like asking the heads of Transport for London to demonstrate they knew every passenger who boarded a train and reached their destination in a safe and timely manner.

This leader believed that, although complex and daunting, the task was achievable, and the journey would make the bank stronger and more resilient to risk. He had an idea of how it might be done, a conviction that it was the right thing to do and the gumption to propose it to the management board. He didn't oversell the probability of success, but he did take personal responsibility for the initiative. It would be his crown jewel—or crown of thorns, as it may be.

The hypothesis, which Priyesh was fortunate enough to be a part of formulating, was predicated on the simple but powerful premise that most people come to work to do a good—if not great—job every day. It suggested that it was systematic gaps in tools and controls that prevented vital information from flowing between the front office and risk managers. If the team identified these gaps with the people responsible for each part of the process and empowered them to enhance their controls, the organization would achieve its goal. If management board members were also given clear information on the integrity of the process and data in their area, they could provide support from the top too.

It was a two-year programme of transformation coupled with a commitment to maintaining the integrity of the risk data process via a quarterly review and attestation by each board member. After a thorough audit, the regulators agreed that substantial improvements had been made to the risk management processes and reduced the bank's capital reserves.

Although the initiative was a huge team effort, the result would not have been achieved without its leader. Not only did he come up with the idea, but he also took significant personal risk to win confidence in it from the management board, the regulator and his team. Furthermore, despite being largely responsible, the reward was one he could share with his team and the organization as a whole.

Trait Three: Asking the Right Questions

A common technique for checking if you understand what someone says to you is to say it back to them in your own words. Some senior leaders have taken this technique further, developing the ability to extract the essence of an argument and add extra focus to it, rather like hitting the auto-enhance wand on a digital photo editor.

We've seen good leaders use it to clarify the direction of travel. They harness powerful but raw ideas generated by their teams, peers and even seniors, and turn them into crisp proposals that can be put into action. While coming up with great ideas are a key attribute for any senior manager, there are limits to how far they will take you. If you're relying solely on yourself for your full stock of ideas, you will eventually run out.

By contrast, if you can take thoughts generated by your team and turn them into clear action plans, you have created a team of thought leaders and multiplied your potential pool of great ideas. It's also a powerful way of motivating your team. Everyone loves to see their brainchild become a reality, particularly when it's played back to them in a clearer, more practical form than they were able to articulate during their initial 'aha' moment. A generous manager will always ensure that, no matter how much of their own skill they contributed to refining the idea, credit is given where it is due.

An interaction along these lines might go as follows:

A team member speaks up in a meeting and highlights an idea. 'We've developed an aggressive plan to deliver this analysis in four weeks. We've set up structured sessions with our technical experts, and although it will be a real challenge given the year-end holiday season, we think we can reach the target if everyone prioritizes it.'

The senior MD comes back with a focused question. 'I agree, this will be challenging given everything else that's going on. Can I ask why we think we need to do this in four weeks?'

'We've been told that the heads of department have discussed the importance of completing the task before year-end so we can start next year with a clear picture.'

The senior MD reframes the response. 'Understood. We're conducting this analysis to have a credible plan at the beginning of next year.'

Then he follows up with another focused question. 'Are there any aspects of this analysis that are more critical for next year's plan than others?'

'Yes, there are more uncertainties in the first two parts of the analysis than the second two.'

Once again, the senior MD reframes the team member's answer. 'So, we should focus more on the first two parts and if the rest slips into January, that would impact our plan less.'

'Yes, but other department heads may not be happy that we haven't completed the exercise as they requested.'

The senior MD responds with another focused question. 'Could we limit the analysis on all parts to only those areas that impact our plan for next year and note anything with longer-term impact for a follow-on analysis?'

'Yes, it's possible, although we may not know what that is until we start the analysis.'

The senior MD reframes one final time and restates the idea as a firm and clear plan. 'Understood. Let's make it clear when we tell department heads about our approach that to set up our plan for next year within this tight timeframe, we'll be taking the following steps. First, we'll prioritize the first two tasks, as they have the potential to affect next year's plan the most. Second, we'll focus on areas that benefit next year's plan and reserve the aspects with longer-term impact for follow-on analysis.'

Through focused questioning and reframing, this leader not only managed to home in on the key priorities and dimensions of the task but also helped frame the scope and messaging to set the team up for success. The alternative might have led to a higher-risk approach, where other senior peers may have been led to believe that the team would produce a wider analysis than practically possible. There could've been great potential for disappointment and questions if this wasn't achieved, despite the team's considerable efforts.

Trait Four: Conveying Guiding Principles

An organization that fosters enthusiasm for progress may succeed in developing a highly motivated staff, but it might be a waste of energy if individual, departmental and political agendas differ too greatly. One way of overcoming this is to ensure all stakeholders are agreed on the fundamental goal being pursued. This adherence to an agreed principle may sound like an obvious step, but it's one that is often overlooked.

The ability to step back and define key principles is a sign of a great leader. It lays out the unarguable truth and establishes boundaries on the scope of an endeavour. It sets out a framework of agreement that can be referred to as a core foundation. Organizations defining their core values to build a cultural framework isn't a new concept. Investment banks adopted it following the financial crisis when it was clear that cultural change was urgently needed—and that it had to be clearly articulated and driven from the top.

It's also a tool we've applied ourselves to ensure an initiative begins with all participants and stakeholders on the same page. The trick is to reverse a common negotiating and conflict resolution technique known as 'bubbling up'. Instead of allowing a common understanding to emerge over time as an initiative progresses, you start it from a position of agreement.

At the peak of the trading boom, Priyesh was put in charge of one of the largest and most complex commodities trading systems in City of London Investment Trust. It was a twenty-four-hour, six-and-a-half-day-a-week trading platform, servicing clients in all major locations across the globe. The big challenge was that it was such a busy and lucrative business that there simply hadn't been an opportunity to properly upgrade the system in many years.

It was creaking with out-of-date technology, and the main vendor responsible for building the platform was reaching the limits of its ability to support it. If the system went down, the bank could lose millions in revenue every day it remained out of action—something had to be done. Convincing stakeholders of this wasn't difficult given the risk associated with a system failure. What was proving challenging was agreeing how much the company was going to do to rectify the situation, what commitment was going to be required, and when the system could be suspended to allow for such a major upgrade. To reach an agreement, the team laid out a set of principles as a guide. They were focused on the need to:

- Minimize disruption to the business
- Upgrade all aspects of the system at one go
- Learn from their own and others' mistakes prior to the upgrade
- Communicate the risk involved to all users
- Expect and prepare for downtime

Some of these principles may seem contradictory, but the team was able to devise an implementation plan that respected all of them. For example, to meet the first three requirements, they took the relatively risky approach of upgrading software, hardware and security at the same time to reduce the need for multiple upgrades and subsequent disruption to the business. However, to achieve this 'big bang' implementation, they had to test each component particularly thoroughly, so they organized three forty-eight-hour 'dress rehearsals' involving the hundred-strong upgrade team.

There was a round-the-clock issue resolution approach. Priyesh sent each of his main project managers to trading hubs in New York, Singapore and London and set up resolution teams so they could work twenty-four hours a day to address any glitches.

Finally, his team communicated extensively with all traders, both to provide training on new system features and manage expectations. A smaller upgrade for a parallel business area had recently left its trading system out of service for nearly two weeks, so the team took appropriate measures to protect the bank prior to the upgrade.

It was a resounding success, with many stakeholders congratulating the team on exceeding expectations. There was no system downtime, and wherever issues did arise, the team worked tirelessly across all time zones to correct them.

Although it may sound like an obvious way of working, senior leaders frequently neglect to ensure key principles are clear and agreed early on. Without this understanding, it's hard for a team to shape an approach that drives success and manages stakeholder perceptions.

Trait Five: User-Friendly Communication

One of the most common traits of successful MDs is the ability to interpret complex technical concepts in layman's terms. Effective leaders can capture the essence of a situation in a straight-talking summary that provides both clarity and direction.

It's harder than it sounds. Many of us have climbed the ladder by building technical knowledge and deep expertise, which tends to bring with it a cargo of specialist terms and acronyms. To speak a different language to the one most appropriate for the technical speciality but describe it effectively requires a shift in perception. It takes empathy with the listener and a feel for the images and vocabulary that will bring the subject to life for them.

A senior managing director Priyesh had the pleasure to work with commonly used the power of comparisons to illustrate his points. On making a case for additional funding to support regulatory projects, instead of saying: *'The Basel Accord will bring about a regulation that requires us to make a significant investment in improving our process controls, or it may deem certain trading products unprofitable from a capital adequacy standpoint—'*

He may have painted a picture to introduce his audience to the concept by saying the following as an introduction that would have made the subject more palatable:

> We have a high-speed train of regulation heading towards us. We can either jump out of the way or jump on board. Better still, we should get into the driver's seat if we can. This will be a big investment, but these really are our only choices.

Senior leaders need to get the facts across in a logical manner—both to support arguments and give context for key decisions. To develop the argument further, the MD in question would have continued to provide facts in the same user-friendly manner. They may have said:

> This new set of rules requires a complete overhaul of the models we use to price our products. If we do nothing, it

could multiply our capital requirements four-fold. If we act, we could reduce the impact to one-and-a-half times or lower. Last time we had a similar but simpler rule change, it took eighteen months to implement and cost us $50 million. We need to do more work, but we need to act quickly because, in two years, we are legally required to be compliant with this regulation. Today, we need to decide whether we can move forward with seed funding of $2 million to mobilize the team. We will come back when we have a better understanding in around three months.

You will notice, the technical content is toned down but the practical impact on the business is clear. The argument is backed up with comparisons, and the decision on how to support the next step is presented in a way that makes sense. There may be a need to delve into the technical reasons why this change may cause such an increase in the capital requirement and cost of business. The accomplished presenter will have all those facts to hand if they need them, although again, in as user-friendly a fashion as possible.

All this requires preparation, but the more senior the audience, the more important it is to ensure the key information gets across. Senior time is limited. Great MDs know that to acquire the organization's trust, they need to communicate in understandable language.

Trait Six: Work and Life Are One

Now that you're in the corner office, you want to stay there. If you burn out—or your staff do—you won't be able to sustain your success. One of the most difficult characteristics of the most successful MDs is how they provide an unwavering commitment to the firm while maintaining a work–life balance. It requires supreme time management, effective delegation, empowerment of teams and a razor-sharp focus on the goal.

Priyesh sacrificed a lot to achieve good commercial results early on in his career but realized along the way that loyalty to the firm didn't have to mean disloyalty in other areas of his life. Of course, there are times where compromise just isn't an option, and senior leaders know exactly when those times are. However, with forward planning and team mobilization, a senior leader can live a life with plenty of space for other priorities like fun and family.

There are two reasons why this trait is vital for a long and successful stint in the corner office and continuing your 'upgrade' journey. First, wider priorities are essential for a healthy, rounded life. They ensure your mind is fresh and nourished with experiences of the world outside the office. It feels good and provides raw material for the creativity and original thinking that serves you so well at work. Workaholics tend to have shorter careers and often lack the perspective a true leader requires when guiding an ambitious business through challenging waters.

The other reason for valuing a healthy balance between work and other aspects of life goes back to our definition of leadership. Leaders are followed but only for as long as followers feel the destination is one they want to reach. A leader who constantly sacrifices their home life sets an example that many won't want to aspire to. Meanwhile, a leader who demonstrates unshakable dedication but enjoys a full life is an enviable role model.

It boils down to the amount of time leaders spend thinking, planning and preparing how they manage their people, work and personal lives. It can be condensed into three steps.

1. Set aside an hour a day to think and plan. Focus not only on what needs to be done but also what should be prioritized and how key tasks should be executed.

2. Keep up regular, one-to-one meetings with your key team members to empower and support action. Scale yourself with effective delegation and collective thinking.

3. Plan your personal life and business commitments as a single process so they complement and support each other and celebrate both.

It's our belief and experience that high-performing MDs strive to be successful in all areas of their lives, and those who approach all these aspects together stand a greater chance of achieving that all-important balance.

There are no hard and fast rules, and what is presented here is a collection of traits you may choose to emulate. Each takes minutes to read but time and experience to master. Practice, curiosity, observation and all the other tools presented here have given us the opportunity to refine our abilities and perform more effectively. We hope they will do the same for you.

Bonus Chapter

Zoomify Your Career

To Zoom or not to Zoom—is that really a question anymore?
It's great working from home, isn't it? So much more flexible,
spending more time on the important things in life rather than on
commutes, chasing train schedules and frustrating traffic jams.

In the world of Yin and Yang, give and take, karma, there is
always a balance. So, what could you be giving up in return for all
these wonderful benefits?

'Not very much' I hear many of you shouting into your
microphones. I spend more time working not less; often longer
hours and unless I'm sleeping, I'm always available.

Well, there is some merit to this line of thinking and yet when
you see someone in the flesh, why is it you connect better with
them? Why do you feel a warmth that you can't experience on
screen? It may be because we are not digital or binary beings rather
we are very much analog. Our eyes, touch and other senses are still

more powerful than any super HD camera. With this it carries an almost sixth sense of connectivity.

So here it is, those who meet in person have the clear advantage of connecting at a more human, natural level than those who remain in virtual worlds. Therefore, granted you can probably work harder, longer hours at home but is it always working smarter?

When it comes to building relationships, understanding and being understood, and being present to read facial expressions, eye contact and shaking hands can make a difference.

Now we're not saying it isn't possible to achieve a promotion working from home, and certainly we haven't seen enough evidence to the contrary, but it does close off channels of communication that inevitably makes it harder.

Other challenges also creep into the equation—the more junior you are the more exposure you need to learn how senior leaders behave so they are effective in an organization. Every organization has a culture, preferred modes operandi or style of behaviour. Aspects of this come across in formal calls but some are more easily observed when senior leaders are speaking to each other informally or behind closed doors.

A thirty-minute Zoom or Teams call where a person speaks for around five to ten minutes may deprive you of that opportunity. Why? This is because conference calls tend to be transactional; there is little room for discussing other topics or context around the topic, which you may be able to do if you bump into someone at the coffee machine or are party to a quick exchange before a meeting.

These are valuable nuggets that take you beyond the transactional agenda and allow you to gain a broader perspective and exchange views with seniors and peers. It also allows you to meet the normal person behind the leader, maybe you see a glimmer of yourself which builds confidence that you are on a similar journey. It could allow you to identify not-so-subtle refinements you can make to your approach.

This is a nourishing developmental opportunity as well as a chance to open doors as you connect with people informally and they see you for the real person you are.

Does this ring a bell? Have you ever bumped into someone and ended up having an interesting and pleasant exchange, deciding to meet up again to follow through? This is 101 of networking and working from home makes it harder as you must take a more formal intentional route.

So, please keep this in mind when you are considering whether to be there in person or in 1080p HD.

There is nothing like the personal touch. Give yourself the killer advantage of your personality, shake someone's hand, look them in the eye, have a coffee together and build a bond that a cold screen can't replicate.

However, as we are going to spend more time on Zoom or Teams or Google Meet, is there an etiquette that can make us more effective?

The Art of Zoom Communication?

As shared earlier, extraordinary communication requires more than ordinary preparation. Here are some vital ingredients that you must consider:

1. Appreciate your audience and let them appreciate you.
2. Tightly frame what you want to say; focus attention.
3. Confirm you've been understood.
4. Connect with people on many different levels.
5. Leave the right impression.

These are based on the core pillars we shared earlier that great communicators use to effectively engage their listeners, with some zoomification!

Appreciate Your Audience and Let Them Appreciate You

It requires more effort to build a bond or bridge with your counterparts on an online call. When we meet face to face or over a coffee, we build initial rapport by talking about mundane things like the weather or the surroundings or through nonverbal actions. In the virtual office, it is still vital to make time to connect but what makes things a lot easier is if everyone has their camera switched on and are not dialled in on a phone only. Now, this isn't rocket science, but a lot of valuable time can be wasted if participants aren't clear if they would prefer it to be a video call with screen sharing.

So zoomification tip number one is, don't be shy when setting up an online business meeting. Specify you'll be logging in via video and would like to share your screen online so, if possible, could others do the same—preferably with cameras on.

This gives everyone an opportunity to see each other, connect in as humanly as possible and, without meaning to be nosey, maybe appreciate a beautiful painting on someone's wall to inject warmth into the conversation. It is a privilege in these times of the virus and beyond that we are openly sharing our homes, so why not take the opportunity to appreciate our abodes.

Cameras on will also help create a virtual atmosphere and mood appropriate for your discussion. If it is a serious topic, you can use both your tone of voice and facial expression as you would do when meeting in person. People can raise their hands or give a thumbs up both physically and virtually.

So, appreciate your audience and let them appreciate you by encouraging cameras on.

Tightly Frame What You Want to Say

We would normally not ramble through a meeting without having some structure or idea of outcome(s). Begin with an end in mind as Stephen Covey has taught us in the *Seven Habits of Highly Effective People*. This is essential during a virtual call as it is harder to have a random brainstorm—as while the technology is good, the screen flipping between different speakers can likely make you motion sick if there's too much of it! Having one person speak at a time in sensible airtime chunks allows the call to flow smoothly.

To achieve this, an anchor such as a presentation deck or a few slides allows you to give frame and shape to the meeting. This is a useful tool we use in face-to-face meetings but it becomes vital to structure a virtual one and when your Wi-Fi causes your voice to cut out or you freeze, your visual slide still ensures key messages are communicated. So, the use of a well-structured deck that captures the essence of what you want to say becomes a very valuable zoomification asset.

Use effective communication methods in your deck:

- What do you really want to say? Have an elevator pitch for every slide.
- Apply the rule of three:
  - o Begin with the most interesting part of your discussion to grab attention and get your foot in the door to engage your audience from the get-go.
  - o Ensure you lead the audience to the next key message(s) in order of importance or key decisions they need to make.
  - o Finally confirm collective understanding or follow-up actions.

Confirm You've Been Understood

It all goes to a bit of a waste if we click 'leave the meeting' and flip to the next call with a different understanding of what was agreed. This is especially important as some online calls auto disconnect. While this keeps us disciplined on time, it is critical that we leave a few minutes to summarize the outcomes and most importantly agree on the next steps or when we meet again.

But to zoomify this, as the clock nears the end, people tend to start thinking about their next call or taking a break before back-to-back meetings. So, try to plan to get to the point of summarizing a collective understanding and what could happen next closer to five to ten minutes before the conclusion rather than two minutes before the end. It is likely given the virtual session some clarifications may be required over points which you thought were crystal clear.

Connect with People on Many Different Levels

This is about understanding what is important to people, their organizations both from a transactional point of view and values perspective. This requires you to focus on the human behind the screen and for you to forget the medium.

But this is also about asking the right questions. Zoom or no Zoom, this is a necessity. We must give adequate time for others to share what is meaningful to them, what's keeping them up at night and build that context if we can into the matte we are putting on the table.

As things can get choppy online, have some prepared questions and observations about their market, organization, and so on. Giving the other person breathing space to air their thoughts makes for a more joined up experience on and offline.

Therefore, although having the PowerPoint presentation to give structure is important, having sections of PowerPoint relief where you actively engage others by switching off the PowerPoint for an open discussion on a topic before reverting, can make it a more interactive and fruitful experience.

As hard as it might be, we need to keep reminding ourselves there is a person(s) on the other side of the call not just a TV screen.

Focus on hearts and minds when asking questions and delivering your message to connect at different levels, for example by addressing people by their name and asking how they feel or if they have any questions.

As a great communicator it is your job to ensure it is a two-way, or with many people, a multi-way channel. Zoomify this by switching off the PowerPoint presentation and moving to cameras only. Set the stage for open questions and discussion, trying to engage as many people as possible in the dialogue.

Leave the Right Impression, as All Impressions Count

A final thought—Warren Buffet, the father of investing, once said:

> Never do anything in life if you would be ashamed of seeing
> it printed on the front page of your hometown newspaper
> for your friends and family to see.

This is still an important perspective to have in your daily life especially now in the world of Twitter, Instagram and recordable video conferences. Take care with what you say and how you come across.

Just because you are on a video call from home doesn't give licence to dress or seem unprofessional. While it may be reasonable to be semi-causal and being in your bedroom while working from home, having a messy bed in the background or wearing a shabby t-shirt wouldn't leave the best impression.

On the contrary, having a tidy background and dressing smartly would support a message that you can be trusted to be a professional ambassador for the brand, wherever you are.

The Not-So-Subtle Steps

In conclusion, all the same principles of good communication apply whether zooming or not; however, we need to take extra care to:

- Be organized to all be on a video call together with cameras on.
- Use a medium, such as structured slides and visuals, to ensure structure, so your key messages are not victim to a drop.
- Leave a little more time than normal for conclusions and agreeing on what comes next—ideally five to ten minutes before the end of the meeting.
- Create airtime and etiquette for others to speak by having relevant questions at the ready and PowerPoint relief.
- Dress well, display well, say well and mean well as all impressions count and can be replayed!

Our Zoom and Teams days are here to stay so we must make the most of them as professional mediums as well as for building rapport. However, quality time in person still cannot be fully replicated virtually, so use this prime time wisely and choose face-to-face over screen interaction whenever you want to build deeper mutual understanding.

Acknowledgements

This book would not have been possible without inspiration from the many extraordinary leaders who were a shining beacon of light to me with their unique real-world leadership approach. They placed confidence in me to learn, perform and reap significant benefits. My sincere gratitude to David Stevens, Kieran Ebbs, Michael McGrath, Zak Martin, Bob Diamond, Anshu Jain, Jason Forrester, Melanie Neal, Jagdeep Gupta, Ram Venkataraman, Konrad Joy, Philip Freeborn, Kevin O'Reilly, Jo Oeschslin, Stuart Lewis, NGS, Christian Sewing, Lee Guy and Tidjane Thiam. Some of their unique approaches are reflected in these pages.

I would like to thank Ashu Chadha for turbo-starting me on this journey and giving me a taste of the vigour that entrepreneurship brings. For Rohit Mehrotra who brought in the name and focus of destination Corner Office. I am grateful to Cydney O'Sullivan, our first publisher who helped frame the real spirit of this book, and to

Ram Venkataraman, a true friend who brought Cydney to us. To Daniel Franklin for encouraging Alasdair and me to embark on this partnership, and of course Alasdair for having faith in my ideas and breathing life into the concepts.

A big thank you to Sachin Sharma from HarperCollins India who inspired and guided the concept and content of this new edition.

Pratik Shah, Anke Raufuss, Milan Mehra, Angelo Roxas, Madhur Mehra, Daniel Britz, Anand Kapur, Vikas Gupta, Ross Mckenzie, Renarta Guy and Melis Pistracher for being there for me as invaluable sounding boards. To my outstanding team members and colleagues who have supported me through my career, standing shoulder to shoulder in all my achievements—this work is a record of our collective success.

Finally to my guru, Swami Muktananda Paramahamsa, who taught me the meaning of true equality and meditation.

Thank you to all!
Priyesh

About the Authors

Priyesh Khanna is a senior banking executive with more than twenty-five years' experience and has worked with some of the world's largest financial institutions, such as Deutsche Bank, Barclays, J.P. Morgan and Credit Suisse. He began his career as an IT programmer and built his way up to the post of managing director by driving transformations in technology, risk management and operations. Khanna is based in London and has extensive experience in building and managing large, diverse and talented teams across the US, Europe and Asia. He is also the creator of Fireside leadership-intensive programmes, which are the foundations of this book.

Alasdair Ross is a journalist and consultant with thirty years' experience as a foreign correspondent and a senior executive and editor at The Economist Group. Ross is currently working on writing projects for several publications, including *The Financial Times* in London. He is a keynote and TEDx speaker in global affairs, economics, strategy and risk. He is also a non-executive director at The Economist Intelligence Unit.

30 Years *of*

 HarperCollins *Publishers* India

At HarperCollins, we believe in telling the best stories and finding the widest possible readership for our books in every format possible. We started publishing 30 years ago; a great deal has changed since then, but what has remained constant is the passion with which our authors write their books, the love with which readers receive them, and the sheer joy and excitement that we as publishers feel in being a part of the publishing process.

Over the years, we've had the pleasure of publishing some of the finest writing from the subcontinent and around the world, and some of the biggest bestsellers in India's publishing history. Our books and authors have won a phenomenal range of awards, and we ourselves have been named Publisher of the Year the greatest number of times. But nothing has meant more to us than the fact that millions of people have read the books we published, and somewhere, a book of ours might have made a difference.

As we step into our fourth decade, we go back to that one word – a word which has been a driving force for us all these years.

Read.

Harper
Collins

HARPER
PERENNIAL

HARPER
BUSINESS

HARPER
BLACK

हार्पर
हिन्दी

HarperCollins
Children'sBooks

HARPER
DESIGN

HARPER
VANTAGE

Harper
Sport